First World War

and Army of Occupation

War Diary

France, Belgium and Germany

21 DIVISION
Divisional Troops
97 Brigade Royal Field Artillery
8 September 1915 - 11 September 1916

WO95/2143/2

The Naval & Military Press Ltd
www.nmarchive.com
Published in association with The National Archives

Published by

The Naval & Military Press Ltd

Unit 10 Ridgewood Industrial Park,

Uckfield, East Sussex,

TN22 5QE England

Tel: +44 (0) 1825 749494

www.naval-military-press.com

www.nmarchive.com

This diary has been reprinted in facsimile from the original. Any imperfections are inevitably reproduced and the quality may fall short of modern type and cartographic standards.

© Crown Copyright
Images reproduced by permission of The National Archives, London, England, 2015.

Contents

Document type	Place/Title	Date From	Date To
Heading	2143/2 97 Brigade Royal Artillery		
Heading	21st Division 97th Bde R.F.A. Sep 1915-Sep 1916		
Heading	War Diary Headquarters, 97th Brigade. R.F.A. (21st Division) September (8.9.15 To 30.9.15) 1915		
Heading	War Diary Of 97th Brigade R.F.A. From 8th September 1915 To 30 Sept. 1915 Volume I Page I-V		
War Diary	Witley	08/09/1915	09/09/1915
War Diary	Havre	10/09/1915	15/09/1915
War Diary	Fletre	16/09/1915	26/09/1915
War Diary	Loos	26/09/1915	30/09/1915
Heading	Appendix To War Diary For Sept. 1915 Details Of Firing 97th Bde R.F.A.		
Miscellaneous	Daily Report	02/09/1915	02/09/1915
Miscellaneous	Daily Report	03/09/1915	03/09/1915
Miscellaneous	Daily Report	04/09/1915	04/09/1915
Miscellaneous	Daily Report	05/09/1915	05/09/1915
Miscellaneous	Daily Report	06/09/1915	06/09/1915
Miscellaneous	Daily Report	07/09/1915	07/09/1915
Miscellaneous	Daily Report	08/09/1915	08/09/1915
Miscellaneous	Daily Report	09/09/1915	09/09/1915
Miscellaneous	Daily Report	10/09/1915	10/09/1915
Miscellaneous	Daily Report	11/09/1915	11/09/1915
Miscellaneous	Daily Report	12/09/1915	12/09/1915
Miscellaneous	Daily Report	13/09/1915	13/09/1915
Miscellaneous	Daily Report	14/09/1915	14/09/1915
Miscellaneous	Daily Report	15/09/1915	15/09/1915
Miscellaneous	Daily Report	16/09/1915	16/09/1915
Miscellaneous	Daily Report	17/09/1915	17/09/1915
Miscellaneous	Daily Report	18/09/1915	18/09/1915
Miscellaneous	Daily Report	19/09/1915	19/09/1915
Miscellaneous	Daily Report	20/09/1915	20/09/1915
Miscellaneous	Daily Report	21/09/1915	21/09/1915
Miscellaneous	Daily Report	22/09/1915	22/09/1915
Miscellaneous	Daily Report	23/09/1915	23/09/1915
Miscellaneous	Daily Report	25/09/1915	25/09/1915
Miscellaneous	Daily Report	26/09/1915	26/09/1915
Miscellaneous	Daily Report	27/09/1915	27/09/1915
Miscellaneous	Daily Report	28/09/1915	28/09/1915
Miscellaneous	Daily Report	29/09/1915	29/09/1915
Miscellaneous	Daily Report	30/09/1915	30/09/1915
Heading	21st Division 97th Bde. R.F.A. Vol 2 Oct 15		
Heading	War Diary Of 97th (Howitger) Brigade. R.F.A. From 1st October 1915 To 30th October 1915 Pages VII To VIII		
War Diary		02/10/1915	31/10/1915
Heading	Appendix To W.D. For October 1915 Details Of Firing 97th Bde R.F.A.		
Heading	Daily Report.	01/10/1915	01/10/1915
Miscellaneous	Daily Report.	02/10/1915	02/10/1915
Miscellaneous	Daily Report.	03/10/1915	03/10/1915

Miscellaneous	Daily Report.	04/10/1915	04/10/1915
Miscellaneous	Daily Report.	05/10/1915	05/10/1915
Miscellaneous	Daily Report.	06/10/1915	06/10/1915
Miscellaneous	Daily Report.	07/10/1915	07/10/1915
Miscellaneous	Daily Report.	08/10/1915	08/10/1915
Miscellaneous	Daily Report.	09/10/1915	09/10/1915
Miscellaneous	Daily Report.	10/10/1915	10/10/1915
Miscellaneous	Daily Report.	11/10/1915	11/10/1915
Miscellaneous	Daily Report.	12/10/1915	12/10/1915
Miscellaneous	Daily Report.	13/10/1915	13/10/1915
Miscellaneous	Daily Report.	14/10/1915	14/10/1915
Miscellaneous	Daily Report.	15/10/1915	15/10/1915
Miscellaneous	Daily Report.	16/10/1915	16/10/1915
Miscellaneous	Daily Report.	17/10/1915	17/10/1915
Miscellaneous	Daily Report.	18/10/1915	18/10/1915
Miscellaneous	Daily Report.	19/10/1915	19/10/1915
Miscellaneous	Daily Report.	20/10/1915	20/10/1915
Miscellaneous	Daily Report.	21/10/1915	21/10/1915
Miscellaneous	Daily Report.	22/10/1915	22/10/1915
Miscellaneous	Daily Report.	23/10/1915	23/10/1915
Miscellaneous	Daily Report.	24/10/1915	24/10/1915
Miscellaneous	Daily Report.	26/10/1915	26/10/1915
Miscellaneous	Daily Report.	27/10/1915	27/10/1915
Miscellaneous	Daily Report.	28/10/1915	28/10/1915
Miscellaneous	Daily Report.	29/10/1915	29/10/1915
Miscellaneous	Daily Report.	30/10/1915	30/10/1915
Miscellaneous	Daily Report.	31/10/1915	31/10/1915
Heading	21st Division 97th Bde. R.F.A. Vol. 3 Nov. 15		
Heading	Appendix To W.D. For Nov. 1915 Details Of Stering 97th Bde R.F.A.		
War Diary	Armentieres	01/11/1915	30/11/1915
Miscellaneous	Daily Report	01/11/1915	01/11/1915
Miscellaneous	Daily Report	02/11/1915	02/11/1915
Miscellaneous	Daily Report	03/11/1915	03/11/1915
Miscellaneous	Daily Report	04/11/1915	04/11/1915
Miscellaneous	Daily Report	05/11/1915	05/11/1915
Miscellaneous	Daily Report	06/11/1915	06/11/1915
Miscellaneous	Daily Report	07/11/1915	07/11/1915
Miscellaneous	Daily Report	08/11/1915	08/11/1915
Miscellaneous	Daily Report	09/11/1915	09/11/1915
Miscellaneous	Daily Report	10/11/1915	10/11/1915
Miscellaneous	Daily Report	11/11/1915	11/11/1915
Miscellaneous	Daily Report	12/11/1915	12/11/1915
Miscellaneous	Daily Report	13/11/1915	13/11/1915
Miscellaneous	Daily Report	14/11/1915	14/11/1915
Miscellaneous	Daily Report	15/11/1915	15/11/1915
Miscellaneous	Daily Report	16/11/1915	16/11/1915
Miscellaneous	Daily Report	17/11/1915	17/11/1915
Miscellaneous	Daily Report	18/11/1915	18/11/1915
Miscellaneous	Daily Report	19/11/1915	19/11/1915
Miscellaneous	Daily Report	20/11/1915	20/11/1915
Miscellaneous	Daily Report	21/11/1915	21/11/1915
Miscellaneous	Daily Report	23/11/1915	23/11/1915
Miscellaneous	Daily Report	24/11/1915	24/11/1915
Miscellaneous	Daily Report	25/11/1915	25/11/1915
Miscellaneous	Daily Report	26/11/1915	26/11/1915

Miscellaneous	Daily Report	27/11/1915	27/11/1915
Miscellaneous	Daily Report	28/11/1915	28/11/1915
Miscellaneous	Daily Report	29/11/1915	29/11/1915
Miscellaneous	Daily Report	30/11/1915	30/11/1915
Heading	97th Bde. R.F.A., Vol 4 XCVII Bde. Diary For Dec., 1915, Is Missing. A.F.B.		
Heading	D/XCVII To 2nd Cdn. Div On 5/12/15 To What Bde		
Heading	21st Divisional Artillery. 97th Brigade R.F.A. January 1916		
War Diary	Armentieres (France)	01/01/1916	31/01/1916
Heading	21st Divisional Artillery. 97th Brigade R.F.A. February 1916		
War Diary	Armentieres (France)	01/02/1916	29/02/1916
Heading	21st Divisional Artillery. 97th Brigade R.F.A. March 1916		
War Diary	Armentieres	01/03/1916	23/03/1916
War Diary	Mav Hazebrouck	24/03/1916	30/03/1916
War Diary	Hazebrouck	31/03/1916	31/03/1916
Heading	21st Divisional Artillery. 97th Brigade R.F.A. April 1916		
War Diary	Daours.	01/04/1916	30/04/1916
Heading	21st Divisional Artillery. 97th Brigade R.F.A. May 1916		
War Diary	Dernancourt	01/05/1916	31/05/1916
Heading	21st Divisional Artillery. 97th Brigade R.F.A. June 1916		
War Diary	Dernancourt	03/01/1916	16/01/1916
War Diary	F 7 b 05 05	17/01/1916	31/01/1916
Miscellaneous	A Form. Messages And Signals.		
Miscellaneous	Reference Instructions For Appendix No. 3		
Heading	21st Divisional Artillery. 97th Brigade R.F.A. July 1916		
Heading	War Diary For July Destroyed By Shell Fire		
Heading	21st Divisional Artillery. 97th Brigade R.F.A. August 1916		
War Diary	Denier	01/08/1916	04/08/1916
War Diary	Wanquetin	10/08/1916	31/08/1916
Miscellaneous	A Form. Messages And Signals.		
Miscellaneous	A Battn		
Miscellaneous	A Battn	01/08/1916	01/08/1916
Miscellaneous	21st. D.A. No. B.M. 45 Instructions For Relief No. 1	31/07/1916	31/07/1916
Miscellaneous	Table "A" 95th. Brigade Group.		
Heading	21st Divisional Artillery. Brigade Broken Up 30th August 1916 H.Q. Staff 97th Brigade R.F.A. 1st To 11th September 1916		
War Diary	Wanquetin	01/09/1916	11/09/1916

2143/2

97 Brigade Royal Artillery

21ST DIVISION

97TH BDE R.F.A.

SEP 1915 - SEP 1916

BROKEN U.P

Brigade disembarked
Havre from England
10.9.15.

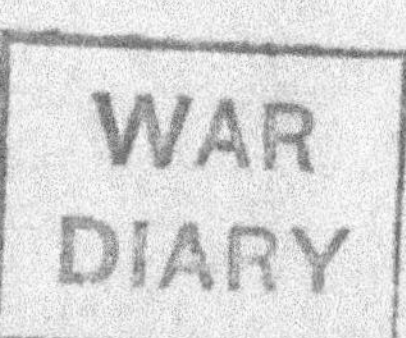

Headquarters,

97th BRIGADE, R.F.A.

(21st Division)

S E P T E M B E R

(8.9.15 to 30.9.15)

1 9 1 5

CONFIDENTIAL

WAR DIARY

of

97th BRIGADE. R.F.A.

from 8th September 1915 to 30 Sept. 1915.

Volume I

pages I–V

Instructions regarding War Diaries and Intelligence Summaries are contained in F. S. Regs., Part II. and the Staff Manual respectively. Title Pages will be prepared in manuscript.

WAR DIARY
or
INTELLIGENCE SUMMARY
(Erase heading not required.)

Army Form C. 2118

I

Place	Date	Hour	Summary of Events and Information	Remarks and references to Appendices
WITLEY	8/9 9 15		The 97 Brigade R.F.A left ~~Witley~~ WITLEY Camp (Surrey) between midnight 8/9 Sept 1915 and noon 9th Sept 1915. Each unit proceeding in separate train H.Q travelling with "A" Bty all entrained at GODALMING. On arrival at ~~Sou~~ SOUTHAMPTON the Brigade embarked under orders of Embarkation officer in 3 boats i.e "MARGUERITE" "NORTH WESTERN MILLER" and BELLEROPHON.	
HAVRE	10 9/15		Arrived at HAVRE at 6 am Disembarkation commenced at 8 am and marched to REST CAMP. The system of disembarking while conducive to speedy clearance was unsatisfactory from a Brigade point of view. as horses, guns, limbers + wagons were all intermixed leading to losses which it was impossible to trace. At this place indents for deficient (un issued) stores were sent to A.O.D but none were available.	
	11 9/15		The Brigade entrained on the 11th and reached St. OMER on the morning of the 12th 9.15 and marched thence to BONNINGUES about 12 miles where it was billetted	
	15 9/15		Brigade marched to ZUYTPEENE about 20 miles	
FLETRE	16 9/15		Brigade marched to FLETRE about 10 miles and went into billets. A certain number of officers and men started on the 17th and were taken by motor busses from METEREN to NIEPPE for attachment to Artillery of XII Division. They all returned on 20 9/15	
	21 9/15		Brigade marched from FLETRE to L'ECLEME and were billetted there.	
	~~24~~ 9/15		Brigade marched from L'ECLEME at 5 30 pm and after 4 hours halt on the way in order to leave road clear arrived about 5 am on 24 9 15 at FOUR-A-CHAUX in drizzling rain a distance of about 14 miles and rested in a field	
	25 9/15		till 1.30 p.m, then marched to NOEUX-LES-MINES in steady rain a distance of about 5 miles. Owing to the congestion on the road	

(they)

1875 Wt. W593/826 1,000,000 4/15 J.B.C. & A. A.D.S.S./Forms/C. 2118.

Instructions regarding War Diaries and Intelligence Summaries are contained in F. S. Regs., Part II. and the Staff Manual respectively. Title Pages will be prepared in manuscript.

WAR DIARY
or
INTELLIGENCE SUMMARY
(Erase heading not required.)

Army Form C. 2118

II

Place	Date	Hour	Summary of Events and Information	Remarks and references to Appendices
	25 9/15		the Brigade did not arrive until 5pm. On arrival Bde Commander received orders to report to R.A. Div H.Q. at once at MAZINGARBE and at 8pm found it at PHILOSOPHE. The Adjt was then sent back to fetch up the Brigade which arrived at 12.15 am 25.9.15. The	
	26 9/15		Brigade bivouacked in a field by side of road until 3am. In the meantime orders were received to send out officers to reconnoitre for positions and get batteries into action by daylight. Four officers went out and reported that they could see nothing and had been sniped at. The O.C. Bde was then ordered to meet G.O.C. R.A. XI Div at 6 am at LE RUTOIRE and after a brief conference rode from there to outskirts of LOOS but owing to mist was unable to see much of the country.	
LOOS	26 9/15		About 9am the four batteries came into action in the open about square G22. Owing to want of information regarding our own infantry, partly due to lack of telephone wire and partly due to Infantry advance having taken place before batteries were brought into action, it was practically impossible to closely support our own Infantry and fire was directed on points behind the main line known to be in the enemy's hands. None of the batteries were provided with trench maps and in consequence information sent back from the front referring to Trench maps was of little use. About 10.30 am D Battery was withdrawn from an exposed position to behind the railway embankment G26 b (Combined sheet 36 1/40.000). About 1pm information was received from a Staff Officer that our Infantry were pursuing the Germans towards PONT-À-VENDIN and required Artillery support. Captain HEATH and Lieut BROOKS were sent forward to reconnoitre for positions and informed that the Brigade would move forward towards LOOS by the LENS Road. When the Brigade approached the rise on the road overlooking LOOS, it was realized that it would be impossible to advance on account of shell fire as owing to trenches on both flanks the batteries were compelled to move in column of route. The batteries were then retired by the adjutant under cover of PUIT No 7. and the C.O. and an officer	

(From)

1875 Wt. W593/826 1,000,000 4/15 J.B.C. & A. A.D.S.S./Forms/C. 2118.

Instructions regarding War Diaries and Intelligence Summaries are contained in F. S. Regs., Part II. and the Staff Manual respectively. Title Pages will be prepared in manuscript.

WAR DIARY
or
INTELLIGENCE SUMMARY

(Erase heading not required.)

Army Form C. 2118

111

Place	Date	Hour	Summary of Events and Information	Remarks and references to Appendices
LOOS	26 9/15		from each battery proceeded towards LOOS by the former German communication trenches. On arriving near the town this party had to turn as the Infantry were falling back by the same trenches. Captain Heath and Lieut Brooks apparently retired soon after and on leaving the trench for the main road were probably caught by machine from the right front as their dead bodies were found soon after. It was then realized that our Infantry instead of advancing were ~~most~~ inclined to face back so batteries were ordered to select positions, dig in during the night and dump ammunition near the guns. This was successfully done. A + B being on the east side of the road (A in square G28 a 9 7 B in square G27 d 9.9) and C + D on the west side behind the railway embankment (both in square G26 c 3 9 to G20 b 3.2) reference Map. BETHUNE COMBINED SHEET. 36a SE 36b NE 36 SW 36c NW 1/40000 2nd Edition. The Bde HQ + wagon lines being in PHILOSOPHE Bde HQ on LENS ROAD (Square G 27 b 3.2) Casualties: 2 Officers Killed (Captain G E HEATH Cdg "C" Bty. 2nd Lieut R St G BROOKS D Bty) 5 NCOs + men wounded. Ammunition Expended Shrapnel 119 rds HE 34 rds.	
LOOS	27 9/15		Batteries still in same position. The choice of observing stations lay between (a) the crest along which ran our former first line trenches, (b) the town or neighbourhood of LOOS (c) the large slag heap of FOSSE No 3 de BETHUNE. At (a) there was no communication with our infantry, (b) view was very restricted among the ruins and owing to the enemy's increasing H.E. and Shrapnel fire none of the standing structures could be utilized (c) was rather far back and nothing could be seen when the weather was misty. By degrees the batteries were linked up with H.Q. (Bde) and later on a wire was kept in more or less working order from LOOS to Bde H.Q. and was one of the chief means of communication from there to 21 D.A. H.Q. On this date the Brigade was transferred to a group under Command of Lieut Col D.R. COATES DSO to assist the GUARDS DIV. In the afternoon the C.O. and Adjutant went to LOOS and consulted with Genl HEYWORTH as regards how the guns could best assist, but as the town was under heavy shell fire and there was no telephone communication with the batteries, they returned about 6 30 pm. The	

1875 Wt. W593/826 1,000,000 4/15 J.B.C. & A. A.D.S.S./Forms/C. 2118.

Instructions regarding War Diaries and Intelligence Summaries are contained in F. S. Regs., Part II. and the Staff Manual respectively. Title Pages will be prepared in manuscript.

WAR DIARY
or
INTELLIGENCE SUMMARY
(Erase heading not required.)

Army Form C. 2118

IV

Place	Date	Hour	Summary of Events and Information	Remarks and references to Appendices
LOOS	27/9/15		The Targets fired at on this and subsequent days were chiefly certain houses near PUIT 14 bis (said to contain machine guns) and searching BOIS HUGO (squares H 25 d to H 26 a, b) & Wood South of it.	
			Casualties:– NIL	
			Amm^n Expended:– H.E. 240 rds Shrapnel:– 221 rds	
			Major Boone assumed duties of Brigade Major 31st Div vice Dobla Killed	
			Capt Ritchie took over Command vice ~~Boone~~	
			Lieut Amoroso from B^de A.C. joined C/97 vice ~~[illegible]~~ HEATH Killed	
			Lieut Smith assumed command of "E"/97 vice Heath Killed	
LOOS	28/9/15		The same targets were engaged this day. Lieut McLaughlin and a party of 6 Telephonists and runners came under a severe shell fire in a trench near LOOS Cemetery. The officer was wounded and all the men with him killed or wounded with the exception of B^r Shimming of "D" Bty, who gallantly went back & forward along some 50 yards of shell swept road to bring stretcher bearers to remove the whole party. His conduct was later brought to the notice of G.O.C. R.A. 31 Div.	
			Casualties: Lieut P.H. McLaughlin. Wounded	
			48760 Cpl. W. Slater. Killed D/97	
			63835 Gr. L. Mandy ~~[illegible]~~ Wounded D/97	
			Lieut C. Martin joined D/97 from D.A.C vice ~~Brooks Killed~~ ~~[illegible]~~	
			Ammunition Expended Shrapnel 62 rds HE 337 rds	
LOOS.	29/9/15		Same targets & positions as 28.9.15	
			Casualties – Nil –	
			Ammunition Expended Shrapnel 38 rds HE 125 rds	
			(Same)	

1875 Wt. W593/826 1,000,000 4/15 J.B.C. & A. A.D.S.S./Forms/C. 2118.

Instructions regarding War Diaries and Intelligence Summaries are contained in F. S. Regs., Part II. and the Staff Manual respectively. Title pages will be prepared in manuscript.

WAR DIARY
or
INTELLIGENCE SUMMARY.
(Erase heading not required.)

Army Form C. 2118.

V

Place	Date	Hour	Summary of Events and Information	Remarks and references to Appendices
LOOS	30 9/15		Same targets and positions as 28 - 29 9 15 On this date C.O. orderly officer and Lieut Bain went up to LOOS at day light to H.Q of 35 Infy Bde which had relieved part of the Guards ~~Brigade~~ Division. On this date (after dark) that part of the line held by the remainder of the Guards Division and subsequently by the ... Infantry Brigades was taken over by French troops. Other junior officers also arrived with the idea of being attached to Infy Battns but owing to lack of telephone gear and inability to reach forward trenches in daylight they were unable to proceed. On the night of the 30-9 to 1-10 half the guns of the brigade were replaced by those of 65 Bde R.F.A and the relief was completed on the night 1-2 October 9 15. The Brigade had brought out from England some 10000 sandbags of which about 8000 were used, these and all Telephone connections were handed over. Casualties Nil Ammunition Expended Shrapnel 26 rds H.E 47 rds	

[signature] Lieut Colonel R.F.A
Commanding 97 Brigade,
Royal Field Artillery

8353 Wt. W2544/1454 700,000 5/15 D. D. & L. A.D.S.S./Forms/C. 2118

Appendice to War Diary
for Sept. 1915

Details of Firing
97th Bde R.F.A.

SEPTEMBER
1915

DAILY REPORT

2/Sept/15

A

TIME	BTY.	no. of rounds fired	TARGET.
4·26pm	119	1	test pt 484. 47 secs.
2pm	120	1	test pt 425, 72 secs
9·15am	120	2	pt 417. Working party.
6·25am	120	2	pt 417. Snipers.

B

~~Following report received at 10.50am on 1st Sept too late for yesterdays report.~~

Daily Report. 3 · 9 · 1915

A/

[T]IME	Bty.	No. of rounds fired	Targets fired at.
[illegible]5 am	U	1	pt. 470.
[illegible]5 am	120th [illegible]	2	pt 417 working party.
15 pm	120"	8	German first line trenches for observation purposes
15 pm	120"	12	"do"
B/			
[illegible]26 pm	4·2 [illegible] fire [illegible] [illegible] wood	[illegible] few	[illegible]

Daily Report. 4 Sept. 1915

A/

TIME.	BTY.	No. of rounds fired.	TARGET fired at:
6.12 pm	A	15	BOIS FAVIERE in retaliation for Germans shelling BOIS le MARICOURT.
3.40 pm	U	3	·437
4 PM	119	16	Q 17, retaliation for Germans shelling our trenches. The gun was firing from this square.
8.5 am	120	2	Snipers post Q 3 1/2. Test by O. P. at group.
2.45 pm	120	10	Checking lines from a new observation post.
4 PM	37	2	·423 in retaliation for Germans shelling our trenches.

B

3.20 pm	L.F. 9	30	our 32 and 33 trenches. from direction of Q 17

Daily Report 5·9·15

A.

TIME	B'ty.	No. of rounds fired	TARGET.
10·30 AM	A	15	Q.11 6/4. aeroplane registration
6·5 pm	A	9	BOIS FAVIERE, retaliation.
9·25 pm	A	6	pts 441—436. at request of Dorset Regt.
B.			
10·10 am	U	5	Q.11, Q 5. aeroplane registration.
10·45 am	119	12 ~~3~~	Q.17. (Q11. Q5) aeroplane registration
12·5 pm	119	7	·481 retaliation to rifle grenades
9. AM	120	3	·412
8. PM	120	1	Snipers post ·417
5·5 pm	120	1	·417
11·AM	37	2 Lyd.	·487. retaliation (germans shelling No 12 trench)
11·AM	37	4 Shrapnel	CHAPEAU de GENDARME. retaliation ~~[illegible]~~
8·30 pm	37	2 Lyd	Q 3 3/3. Rifle fire sounded from this direction.

B.

TIME	B'ty.	No. of rounds fired	TARGET.
10·45 am	4·2. How	- - - - - -	MOULIN de FARGNY from direction R 19 6/2.
12·20 pm	- - - - - -	- - - - - -	about Q 8 7/5
2·30 pm	LFG	3	fired over BOIS de MARICOURT
5·50 pm	4·2 How.	- - - - - -	behind 29 trench.
9·52 pm		6	near trench 87
~~[illegible]~~	~~4·2 How~~	~~6~~	~~BOIS de MARICOURT~~

Daily Report. 6-9-15.

A.

TIME.	BTY.	No. of rounds. fired.	TARGET.
8.30am	A	6	BOIS FAVIERE retaliation.
12.10pm	U	11	Barricades on PERONNE RD. pts 462-464
2.5pm	U	6	aeroplane registering
10.30am	119	10	Q 24 5/2 1/2, german observing post
11.0am	119	5	Fresh work on trench near 487
2.5pm	119	3	aeroplane registering
10.10am	120	5	Working party pt 417.
11.15am	120	12	BOIS FAVIERE, retaliation.
11.30am	120	10	Q3 8/2. working party.
11.45am	120	5	Q10 2/9. trenches near pt 433.
11.AM	37	6	on a party of germans in BOIS du CHAPITRE
2.14PM	37	5 HE	Q16 4/4. new german dugouts.

B.

TIME.	BTY.	No. of rounds. fired.	TARGET.
8.30am	L.F.G	6	BOIS de MARICOURT. from N.E
11.45am	4.2 how		do
4pm	L.F.G	16 (6. [illegible])	our trench mortar in 35 trench from the north

Daily Report 7/9/15

A.

TIME	Bty	No. of rounds fired	TARGET
10.15am	A	9	BOIS d'en HAUT. Retaliation
11.40am	U	3	Train on railway line. N 17 9/4 (The range was too long)
3.45pm	U	3	working party M 35 4/2
2.50pm	119	5	Q 23 7/0 working party.
9.45am	120	6	opposite 28 trench. Retaliation
1.20pm	120	8	opposite 28 trench.
2.50pm	120	2	Communication trench pt 436. registering
10.40am	37	6. HE	German guns 6319 and 6219. R25. Retaliation
1.30pm	37	4. HE	do. do.
10pm	37	2 HE	Working party at pt 481.

B.

.30am	L.F.G	30	Bois de Maricourt. From direction of ~~R.25. HE~~ R.25
30am	4.2	50	gun at Frise from direction of R.25
1.25am	4.2	7	gun at Frise from about Q 30 9/9

Adjt [illegible] Lt
Adjt. RA Group

Daily Report 2/9/15

A.

TIME	B'ty	No. of rounds fired	TARGET.
2.15pm	A	6 HE S.S.	pt 436. [illegible]. Two direct hits.
6.2pm	A	8 [illegible]	BOIS FAVIERE. retaliation
	U		
2.20pm	119	8 2 HE	pt 5131. enemy's guns.
2.30pm	119	8 2 HE	pt 5811 enemy's guns.
4 PM	119	8 1 HE	pt 457. working party.
10.25am	120	4	pt 417 & pt 436
3.45pm	120	12	~~[illegible]~~ M 34 7/7. On the road.
3.15pm	120	6	M 34 7/7 First line trenches .417 to 430
3.35pm	120	3 HE	pt 417. Two very effective on parados.
7.23am	37	2 HE	pt 464. at request of infantry.
12.30pm	37	1 HE	pt 487. This round fell into enemy's trench.
1 pm	37	4 HE	pt 473 - pt 478
5.35pm	37	7 HE	north of pt 441. Testing line from new gun pits.
~~3.35pm~~	37	~~7~~ HE	~~at wood Q 16 5/3 in conjunction with infantry trench mortar.~~
9.15pm	37	2 HE	Wood Y
[illegible]			
1.20pm		6	Q16 1½/3½
6PM	L.F.G	30	S.E. corner of MARICOURT wood.
9.[illegible]pm	LFG	6	~~[illegible]~~ Q16 2/2. From the East.

[illegible] Capt
Capt RA group

Daily Report. 9/9/15.

A.

TIME.	BTY.	No. of rounds fired	TARGET.
12.45pm	"A"	5	BOIS FAVIERE.., Retaliation.
12.25pm	"U"	12	pt 457. German observation party.
	U	7 S. 8 HE }	South of pt 457. artillery observing station
5 pm	U	23	Trenches in 'A' Bty's zone. Q10 2/7, 441, 443.
	U	6	pt 457. Fired at intervals during the night.
1.55 pm	119	3	Q22 9/5. Working party.
2.15 pm	119	2	Q23 1/6 Working party.
5.15 pm	119	4	pt 487. Retaliation
5.35 pm	119	10	~~[illegible]~~. new communication trench Q22 8/5
3.30 pm	119	4	chapeau de gendarme
5.45 pm	119	3 HE	do
5.45 pm	119	2	Q22 8/5
6.20 pm	119	3	Q22 8/5
6.55 pm	119	3	do
5.25 pm	120	9	pt 417. 2nd line trench.
6.33 pm	120	8	German wood. Retaliation
3.0 pm	37	17	'457 Working party
6.8 pm	37	1 HE	Y wood
6.43 pm	37y	2 HE	German wood. Working party
~~10.0 pm~~	37	1 HE	Y wood.

B.

TIME.	BTY.	No. of rounds fired	TARGET.
12.40pm	LFG		23 Support trench
3.10pm	L.F.G	~~4~~ 20	Trench 13 from direction of R19
2.45pm	L.F.G	10	Maricourt wood.
5.45pm	LFG	8	do
6.20pm	bombs	4	Q9 3/3, Q6 8/6

[illegible signature] for

adjt RA group

Daily Report. 10-9-15

A.

TIME	BTY	No. of rounds fired	TARGET.
9.30am	A	13	Observation Post in BOIS FAVIERE and trenches 441–448
8.40pm	A	5	Working party. pt 436.
5.30pm	U	2	observing station near pt 457. one direct hit
5.35pm	U	5	working party Q 5 1/5
7 PM	119	3	Q 22 8/5. working party. Work stopped.
8.50pm	119	3	working party at Q 22 8/5.
10.45pm	119	3	do.
3.5am	119	1	Y wood. Q16 4/3
10.50 am	120	5	Trenches at pt 412
1.12 pm	120	2	pt 423
5.45 pm	120	2	pt 417 working party.
9.40 pm	37	3	Y wood Q16 4/3
1.40 am	37	2	pt 467. working party

B.

7.50am	4.2 How	6	119th Bty position from direction of Q18 3/2 or Q18 8/4.

[signature]
Adjt R1 Group

Daily Report. 11/9/15.

A

TIME.	Bty.	No. of rounds fired	TARGET.
1.45 pm	U	2	pt. 457
4.30 am	U	5	Q 5 10/5. Working party.
12.55 pm	U	2	pt. 467
12.55 pm	U	10	Trenches between 436 and 448
4.5 pm	U	5 S 2 HE }	pt 467 Working party
5.10 pm	U	4	5131. Q 18. retaliation.
~~3.5 am~~	~~119~~	~~+~~	~~Working party & wood~~
10.36 am	119	5	5132. Q 18. retaliation.
3.5 pm	~~2~~ 119	5 2 HE }	Q 23 9/3. Haystack.
3.20 pm	119	5	5131. Q 18 retaliation.
4.30 } 5.15	119	10	5131. 5132 retaliation.
3.30 pm	120	12	pt. 417.
4.50 pm	120	4	pt. 417
5.15 pm	120 ~~6 S 3 HE~~ }	6 S 3 HE	M 33 5/2
5.40 pm	37	2 HE	Chapeau working party.
B.			
8 am	4.2 how	26	Dummy battery at Q 26 5/5. (These rounds were not reported yesterday)
5.30 pm	4.2 in How	~~3~~ 6	Q 8 7½/5.
5 pm	E.F.G.	12	Q 15 6/4. Ground scored D como ~~[illegible]~~ from Q 18 2/2

Daily Report. 12/9/15

A

TIME	B'ty	No. of rounds fired	TARGET
4 PM	U	15	Working party Q.16 3/4
5.15 PM	U	10.S 4 HE	pt 457. A probable M.G. emplacement.
12.30 am	U.	3	pt 457
2.36 PM	119	4	Working party. Q 22 1/3.
2.45 PM	119	2	"do"
7.25 PM	119	2	"do"
12.55 pm	120	3	Test pt 432. 2 mins
3.25 am	120	3	pt 417
5.30 pm	120	9	Q 9 5/8. Retaliation. 5 rounds effective on 1st line trenches
6.0 pm	120	10	BOIS. FAVIERE. Retaliation. Germans shelling MARICOURT Wood.
~~9.30 pm~~	~~120~~	~~1~~	
9.30 pm	120	1	pt 430. test. 10 secs
9.24 am	37	5	Q12. 5540. Hostile battery position.
4.28 PM	37	5 Lyd	.436
4.30 PM	37	1 Lyd	CHAPEAU. Working party. Work was stopped.
10.30 pm	37	2 Lyd	.431. Working party spotted by infantry.
B.			
7 to 8.30 am	4.2	abt 80	Anti-aircraft gun in valley Q19.
5.15 PM	L.F.G	812	MARICOURT. wood. from direction of Q18 2/2
5.52 PM	F.F.G	6	"do"

W. J. Gollum [?] Lieut
adjt Rt group

Daily Report. 13 9/15

A.

TIME	BTY.	No. of rounds fired	TARGET.
9.15am	A	3S 6 HE }	pt 443. Working party.
1.30am	U	2 HE	·457
8pm	U	3	·462. working party
0 am	119	10	Railway Station Q11 5/4
·25pm	119	31	Wire in front of 487 to 481 and 467 to 484.
0 am	120	12	Railway Station Q11 5/4
·45pm	120	28	Wire in front of pt 430.
·3pm	120	2	test pt 415. 60 secs
·35pm	120	7	german observation party Q9 1/2/9
·35pm	120	1	test pt 4[illegible], time 8 secs.
·55 am	37	13 HE	pt 464

B.

1PM	4·2	·12	Q16 2/4

[illegible] A
[illegible] Gp.

Daily Report 14/9/15

A.

TIME	BTY	No. of rounds fired	TARGET.
8·30am	A	4	pt 448. Working party.
8·30am	A	2	pt 448. Working party.
1·25 pm	A	12 S 2 HE	pt. 450. Retaliation. Request of 14th Inf. Bde.
5 PM	U	2	Verifying points for O.P. A/98 Bty.
1·40AM	U	4	Working party pt 481
4·10pm	119	6	pt 484. Working party.
8·30am	120	4	pt 425. Working party
10·15am	120	2	pt 423. Working party. Fire very effective.
3·10pm	120	2	pt 428. Test. 60 secs
3·30pm	120	18	trenches from 428 to 430.
10·30pm	120	1	test pt 423 .40 secs.
during the night	120	10	1st line trenches between 428 – 430
10·50am	37 ~~2 L~~	2 L	pt 448. Working party
3 pm	37	3 L	Q 16 5/5
2·45 pm	37	7 L	trenches from pt 428 to pt 430. Considerable damage.
5·15 pm	37	2 L 2 S	working party. M 35 10/6

B.

TIME	BTY	No. of rounds fired	TARGET.
1·47pm	LFG	6	No 2/2 trench. Reported by 14th Inf Bde.

Daily Report 15/9/15

A

TIME.	Bty.	No of rounds fired	TARGET.
1.40 am	U	4	pt. 461. Working party.
3 PM	U	2	pt. 445.
12.40 PM	119	5	Q 2 6/3 working party
2.50 PM	119	6	Q 22 7/4 do
3.5 PM	119	2	Q 22 7/4 do
3.15 PM	119	2	Q 22 7/4 do
1.35 am	119	3	
8.15 am	120	4	pt 423
12.30 PM	120	8	Q 3 3/7. German wire on 3rd line trenches
2.35 PM	120	1	test pt 428. 30 secs.
11.35 PM	120	1	test pt 423 15 secs.
1.25 am	120	2	Working party pt 423
12.30 PM	A/98	29	registering pts in area
12 30 PM	D/98	31	registering pts in area.
6.10 PM	37	3 L	Working party. pt 487
B			
1 PM	42		PERONNE. Road

[illegible] Lt

Capt RA group

Daily Report. 16/9/15.

A.

TIME	B'ty.	No. of rounds fired	TARGET.
11.35 am	119	12	Q 24 5/0. German dug outs
3.10 pm	119	12	new trench Q 22 9/5
4.15 pm	119	1	Listening post CHAPEAU de GENDARME
1.25 am	120	2	pt. 423
3 pm	180	125 (5 HE)	Q 9 7/9 enemy's loop holes. Very effective.
3.45 pm	122		
12.45 am	120	1	~~pt~~ 423. 45 secs.
3.30 pm	A/98	~~#~~ 30	Registering area.
3.30 pm	D/98	24 ~~35~~	Registering area.
8.10 am	37	3 L	Q 22 8/0. working party.
6.50 pm	37	5 L (2 blind)	CHAPEAU de GENDARME. To stop rifle grenading.

B.

10.30 am	4.2	1	From direction of S 427 - fell near ~~R~~ Q 24 5/5.

[illegible] Lieut. R.A.
Adjt. R.A. Group.

Daily Report 17 9/15

A

TIME	B'y	No. of rounds fired	TARGET.
12·30pm	119	11	Q 23 6/7, Q 22 8/6, Q 22 9/8, Q 21 1/6.
12·25pm	120	1	Test pt 423 50 secs
5·25pm	120	1	Test pt 428 43 secs
11·30pm	120	8	On railway. M 33 8/5. Devons reported a train at this point.
11·9PM	120	1	Test pt 423. 65 secs.
8·40am	37	1 Lyd	Q 22 9/8. Working party
9·10am	37	1 Lyd	Q 22 9/8 " " . Hit the parapet.
4·15pm	37	2 Lyd	Q 16 4/4 "
3·5pm	37	5. S	Chapeau de Gendarme. Working party.
3·45pm	37	12 Lyd (4 blind)	Q 10 3/3.

B.

11·30am		2	NE corner of Q 32 from direction of MAUREPAS
4·20pm			Q 15 9/8 from direction of 4534 Q 17

Lt J [illegible] Alun [illegible]
Adjt RA group

Daily Report. 18/10/15

A.

TIME	B'ty.	No. of rounds fired	Target.
3.40 PM	119	2	BOIS de HEM. Retaliation.
6.0 PM	119	3	Bois Y
12.20 pm	120	8	Brickery. M33 Retaliation
11.30 am	123	36	Registering.
11.45 am	124	2	Registering.
12 30 pm	124	32	Registering
5.20 pm	37	3	Bois Y. Considerable movement and work.

B.

12.15 PM	LFG	~~2~~ 4	Q 8/6 from direction of BOIS BERNAFAY
3.35 PM		2	BOIS de VAUX 5 5 40 Maurepas.
2.40 PM	Shrapnel	10	MARICOURT wood from direction of ~~MARICOURT~~
5.30 PM	Light HE	7	Q 16 3/6. (our lap)

[illegible signature]
adjt RA. Group

Daily Report. 19/9/15.

A.

TIME	Bty.	No. of rounds fired	TARGET.
4.30PM	119	4	CHAPEAU de GENDARME. party of germans
10.10 PM	119	3	Wood Y
11.30 PM	119	3	wood Y
12.30PM	119	3	wood Y
8.50am	120	1	pt 430 working party.
9.14am	120	2	"do"
10.23am	120	1	test ·430. 50 secs
4.15 PM	120	3	Q 9 4/2/9½.
11 am	123	23	registering.
3.50 PM	123	6	registering. pt 450
3.30PM	124	8	registering, right and left of ·475
9.25PM	124	8	·464 } Retaliation.
9.25PM	124	4	Bois d'en Haut } Retaliation.
12.15 PM	37	6 HE	Bois Y.
12.40 PM	37	9 HE	·430
12.20 PM	37	6 HE	Southern end Y wood
3.10 PM	37	1 HE	·487. One officer and 8 men showed themselves over parapet
3.30PM	37	13 HE	·487
10.20pm	37	13 HE } 2 S }	BOIS Y. in conjunction with 119th Bty.
2.0 am	37	4. HE	·487. Retaliation to trench mortar. Believed effective.

B.

TIME	Bty.	No. of rounds fired	TARGET.
11.40am		8	in front of 120th Bty from direction of M26
9.15PM			Maucourt Wood and trench 19, reported by infantry.

W.J. Allen ?
Adjt. Rt. Group

Daily Report 20/9/15

A

Time	Bty.	No. of rounds fired	TARGET.
10.30 am	119	5 HE	Haystack observation post Q 23 3/3.
11.45 am	119	5 HE	point 487
12.35 pm	119	9	FERME ROUGE. Hostile Batteries. Retaliation.
10.30 am	120	5 HE 5 S	pt 417. Snipers gallery.
12.25 pm	120	12	Brickerie M 33. Retaliation
12.5 pm	120	5	423 Retaliation.
[illegible] pm	120	15	[illegible]
[illegible] pm	120	10	pt 430. Working party
7.30 am	120	6	Brickery. retaliation
[illegible] 30 pm	123	7 –	Registering near pt 443
[illegible] 0 pm	123	5 –	pt 443
0.10 am	124	6	Working party. Q 16 5/4. Work was stopped
4.0 pm	124	25	registering area
1.55 am	37	1 S	BOIS BERNAFAY
2.30 pm	37	4 HE	5540. Q 12. Hostile Batteries. Retaliation.
[illegible].10 pm	37	3 S 1 HE	( )
2.15 am	37	5	Trench Mortar. S end of Y wood. Mortar stopped firing after 6 rds.

B

Time	Bty.	No. of rounds fired	TARGET.
[illegible].40 am		20	Q 19 8/5
2.10 pm	LFG	15	BOIS de MARICOURT from direction of Q 6.
2.30 pm	LFG 4.2	30 32	Q 8 9/3 from direction of MONTAUBAN
[illegible].30 pm	LFG.	8	BOIS de MARICOURT, from direction of Q 6.
[illegible]30 am	LFG 4.2		No 37 Bty position from direction of MAUREPAS

[illegible]
Capt [illegible] group

Daily Report. 21-9-15.

A.

Time	Bty.	No. of rds. fired	TARGET
[illegible]	[illegible]	[illegible]	
3 PM	119	12	Q 23 8/3, Q 22 7/4
9.35 PM	119	10	Train in HARDECOURT Stn.
11.30 PM	119	8	Y wood
12.30 am	119	8	Y wood
4 PM	120	15	Q 3 4/8½. gun emplacement.
9.45 PM	120	2	428. German Patrol reported by infantry.
7.30 am	120	6	Battery. retaliation
12.5 PM	123	16	Registering 124th Bty Zone.
10.20 am	124	6	Working party Q. 17 5/8.
5.30 PM	124	20	Registering various points.
3.45 PM	37	15 } 5 HE }	M 35 2/2. Observation post. on the farm. 3 direct hits
9.20 PM	37	4 HE	Train in HARDECOURT. Stn.

B.

Time	Bty.	No. of rds. fired	TARGET
7am to 7.30 am	LFG 42 5.9	about 80	Q 31 9/10. From direction of Q18 5838. or Q12 5540.

Daily Report 22.9.1915.

A.

Time.	Bty.	No. of rounds fired	TARGET.
3.45 PM	119	10	Y wood. in conjunction with 37th Bty
11.15 am	120	6	BOIS FAVIERE. Retaliation. Request of infantry.
5.15 PM	120	6	pt 430. Retaliation to ~~[illegible]~~ rifle grenades.
3.15 PM	123	24	Registering 120th Bty zone
5 PM	123	10	.457. Retaliation to Germans shelling. 19.20.21 trenches request of 14th Inf. Bde.
3.30 PM	124	12	pt 464. in conjunction with 37 Bty
4.40 PM	124	12	Registering
3.30 PM	37	20 HE (13 blind)	Q 16 5/5
B.			
11.0 AM	LFG		Shelled 28 and 29 trenches. from direction of NE.
3.30 PM	LFG	2	Q16 3/3
4.40 PM	4.2	20	19.20.21. trenches (Very high bursts)

A.J. Allen Lt
Adjt Rt. Group.

Daily Report. 23.?.6.

A.

Time	Bty.	No. of rounds	TARGET.
8.30am	120	3	Working party Q 2 9/1
11.0am	120	20	·428 to ·430. also railway through BOIS de BERNAFAY.
5.10am	120	4	·430.
	~~123~~		
11.55am	124	16	·457 ·462 } Retaliation. Rifle grenades on 18·19·20 trenches
12.0PM	124	12	·457 }
3.20PM	124	15	BRICKERIE (M 33)
7.50PM	124	8	working party on trenches N of PERONNE Rd, demolished by 37th Bty (yesterday)
9.5PM	124	16	pt. ·457. Retaliation. Germans ~~shelling~~ shelling 19-20. trenches ~~[illegible]~~
10.00am	37	12 HE	aeroplane registration.
4.0PM	37	4 HE	"do"
9.5PM	37	4 HE	N end of Y wood. Retaliation. Germans shelling 19·20. trenches.

B.

9.PM	LFG		19 and ~~20 trenches~~. Reported by 14 Inf. Bde.

Daily Report 25 9/15

A.

Time	Btty	No. of rounds fired	TARGET
	119		
12.0pm	120	3	423- 428
2.0PM	120	3	423- 428
	123		
2.25PM	124	3	observation post ·457
3.5PM	124	6	working party ·467
4.15PM	37	10 HE	BOIS ALLEMAND
4.30PM	37	8 HE	Brisking. M33.
7.5PM	37	12 HE	·464
7.8PM	37	5 HE	Y wood.
2.0PM	37	2 HE	Wood Q 3 3/3

B.

Daily Report 26 9/15

A.

Time	Bty.	No. of rounds	TARGET.
2 PM } 4 PM	119	22 HE } 10 S	Listening post and comm: trench at foot of CHAPEAU.
4.45 pm	119	12	1 salvo. following by 2 salvos at 4.50 pm
2 PM	120	20 HE	Brickery. M 33
2.30 PM	120	50.	Wire between 423-428
3.15 PM	120	10	363-407. registering
4.45 PM	120	12	1 salvo followed by two salvos at 4.50 pm.
During night	120	8	Wire 423-428.
8 am	120	6	423-428. enemy rifle grenading.
2.30 PM	123	20 HE } 15 S	436. 443. and wood Q10 8/4.
4.45 PM	123	12	1 salvo followed by 2 salvos at 4.50 pm.
2 PM	124	20 HE } 15 S	Comm: trench east of .473.
4.45 PM	124	12	1 salvo followed by 2 salvos at 4.50 pm.
6.20 PM	124	4 HE } 6 S	pt. 455 retaliation.
2.15 PM	37	54 (35) HE	pts. 428-430-481.
7.55 AM	37	4 HE	pt. 428 enemy rifle grenading.

B.

Time	Bty.	No. of rounds	TARGET.
1.45 pm	LFG	8	13 and 14 trenches.
2.50 pm	LFG	16	13 and 14 trenches
3.30 pm	LFG	6	do.
4.50 pm	LFG		Machine gun wood. Q8 8/6., trenches 30. 31. 32
4.50 pm	4.2	4	Peronne Road.

[illegible signature]
Capt RA Group

Daily Report. 27 9/15

A.

Time.	Bty.	No. of rounds	TARGET.
8. 3·23 PM	119	3	CHAPEAU. Working party.
8·20 PM	119	2 HE	Comm: trench Q 22 9/8½. Working party at request of 14th Inf. Bde.
9·15 PM	119	2 HE	Working party ·481. at request of 14th Inf Bde.
8·0 am	120	6	423 – 428
4·20 PM	120	1	Snipers post. Q 9 ½/9½.
8·8 PM	120	2 HE	·430. Retaliation.
	123		
4·30 PM	124	4	·464. Retaliation: trench mortars.
5·45 PM	122	5 HE	Trenches just N of PERONNE Rd.
5·30 PM	124	4	·464. Retaliation for trench mortars.
7·35 PM	124	2 HE	·464. ~~Retaliation~~. Working party. Request of 14th Inf. Bde.
8·40 PM	1??	2	Test pt 467
8·0 am	37	4 lydd	·428.
4·45 PM	37	10 lydd	Armoured train M 33 6/4.
6·5 PM	37	2 lydd	Retaliation to trench mortars
6·40 PM	37	2 lydd	·464. Retaliation. Trench mortar. Request of DPLI.
7·45 PM	37	2 lydd	·464 "do"

B.

4·30 pm	42	2	Peronne Rd. Comm: ~~trench~~.

W J Allen Lt
adjt Rt group

Daily Report. 28 9/15

A.

TIME	BTY.	No. of rounds fired.	TARGETS.
		Nil	

B.

		Nil	

Daily Report. 29 9/15

A.

Time	Bty.	No. of rounds fired	TARGET.
			Nil

B.

Time	Bty.	No. of rounds fired	TARGET.
5.45	LFG	1	BOIS de VAUX.

<u>Daily Report 30 4/15</u>

A

Time.	Sh.	No. of rounds fired	TARGET.
11.45 AM	124	4	Work in Q 10 6 ½/4. Retaliation.
9.15 pm	37	5 HE	pt. 481. To stop enemy's trench mortar.
B.			
11.40 am	L F G	15	MARICOURT WOOD. from direction of R 25 5½/1

[illegible] Lt
Adjt RF Group.

21st Division

121 / 7595

97th Bde: R.F.A

Vol 2

Oct 15

CONFIDENTIAL

WAR DIARY

of

97th (Howitzer) Brigade R.F.A.

from 1st October 1915 to 30th October 1915

pages VII to VIII

Instructions regarding War Diaries and Intelligence Summaries are contained in F. S. Regs., Part II. and the Staff Manual respectively. Title pages will be prepared in manuscript.

WAR DIARY
or
INTELLIGENCE SUMMARY.
(Erase heading not required.)

Army Form C. 2118.

Place	Date	Hour	Summary of Events and Information	Remarks and references to Appendices
	2/10/15		Brigade bivouacked near the wagon lines. A stray shell in the night destroyed a water cart and an empty ammunition wagon, 3 men of C/97 were wounded during the day.	
	3/10/15		Brigade marched three miles and bivouacked in square L. 8. d 5.5	
	4/10/15		Brigade marched to MERVEILLE and went into billets 14 miles	
	5/10/15		Brigade marched to HAZEBROUCK and went into billets	
	6/10/15		Brig. Gen Wellesley assumed command of 21st Div Art. 2Lt Lodge and Bland joined from England and were posted to D. Battery and Bde A.C	
	7/10/15		Capt Mc Leod joined from 49th Battn and took over command of C/97.	
	9/10/15		2Lieut Bland transferred from BAC to D/C 2Lieut Amoroso from D to B.A.C	
	10/10/15		Right Sect. A Battery proceeded to Houplines in relief of A 65	
	12/10/15		Left Sect A Battery joined up with right section. This battery was then placed under orders of G.O.C 50th Div. The remainder of the Brigade was inspected dismounted by G.O.C 21st Division, before whom 2Lieut Hon L. U. Kay-Shuttleworth and Driver Shimmin were brought as having done especially good work at Loos	
	20/10/15		Half of B and C Batteries marched to Houplines in relief of Howitzer Batteries of 50th Northumbrian Divn. The O.C and O.O also went on behalf of H.Q	

8353 Wt. W2544/1454 700,000 5/15 D. D. & L. A.D.S.S./Forms/C. 2118.

V11

Army Form C. 2118.

Instructions regarding War Diaries and Intelligence Summaries are contained in F. S. Regs., Part II. and the Staff Manual respectively. Title pages will be prepared in manuscript.

WAR DIARY
or
INTELLIGENCE SUMMARY.
(Erase heading not required.)

Place	Date	Hour	Summary of Events and Information	Remarks and references to Appendices
	22/10/15		Brigade A.C proceeded to Armentiers and billeted near the Peoples Park which is used as a horse lines for the Brigade	
	23/10/15		The remainder of H.Q and B + C Batteries arrived at Houplines These batteries expended 28 lyddite shells in registering.	
	24/10/15		Taking over from 4th Northumbrian F.A Brigade completed. As they had 5 in Hows a certain amount of alteration was necessary for 4.5 in Howitzers. 6 lyddite expended	
	25/10/15		The batteries for tactical purposes were attached as follows: —	
			A to 95th Bde R.F.A	
			B to 94th " "	
			C to 95th " "	
	26/10/15		Expended ammunition 21 lyddite	
	27th/10/15		Ammunition expended. 7 Shrapnel. 51 lyddite	
	28th/10/15		Ammunition expended. 60 lyddite	
			Ammunition expended 28 lyddite	

2353 Wt. W2544/1454 700,000 5/15 D. D. & L. A.D.S.S./Forms/C. 2118.

VIII

Army Form C. 2118.

WAR DIARY
or
INTELLIGENCE SUMMARY.
(Erase heading not required.)

Instructions regarding War Diaries and Intelligence Summaries are contained in F. S. Regs., Part II. and the Staff Manual respectively. Title pages will be prepared in manuscript.

Place	Date	Hour	Summary of Events and Information	Remarks and references to Appendices
29 10/15	29th 10/15		Ammunition expended 12 Lyddite	
	30 10/15		Ammunition expended 1 Shrapnel. 17 Lyddite.	
	31st 10/15		Ammunition expended 13 Lyddite	
			The position of the batteries are as follows.	
			A. C.20.d. 8 8	
			B. C 27.a 8.8	
			C. I.9.c 5.9	
			D. Battery remaining in billets near Hazebrouck.	

[signature] Lt Col
Comdt. 97th Bde R.F.A.

2353 Wt. W2544/1454 700,000 5/15 D. D. & L. A.D.S.S./Forms/C. 2118.

Appendix to W.D. for
October 1915

Details of firing
97th Bde R.F.A.

OCTOBER
1915

Daily Report 1/10/15.

A.

Time	Bty.	No. of rounds fired	TARGET.
9.10PM	119	4	pt 481. Request of 14th Inf Bde. Retaliation
11.0PM	119	3	pt. 481. Retaliation.
~~[illegible]~~	~~[illegible]~~	~~[illegible]~~	~~pt 481~~
8.36PM	37	5 HE	pt 481. request of 14th Inf Bde. Retaliation.

B.

[illegible] Lt
Adjt Rt. Group

Daily Report 2 10/15

A

Time	Bty	no of rounds fired	Target
1.35am	119	6	Chapeau. Retaliation.
2.35am	119	4	Chapeau. Retaliation.
.25am	119	4 S } 4 HE }	chapeau Retaliation. Request of 14th Inf Bde
1.45am	119	6	Chapeau. Enemy shelling our trenches. Request 14th Inf. Bde.
.15PM	119	3 HE	Southern end of Y wood. Retaliation. Request of 14th Inf Bde
1.53pm	120	6 S	.428 Retaliation
.23pm	120	3 S	Bois BERNAFAY
1.0pm	120	5 S	.417 "
1.5pm	120	4 S	BOIS ALLEMAND. "
0.45am	123	6	pt 443 "
11.10am	124	4	pt 455 "
2.20am	124	4	Barricades PERONNE Rd. "
11.35am	37	3 HE	pt 455 "
12.10PM	37	2 HE	Barricades PERONNE Rd. "
2.5 PM	37	7 HE (2 blind)	machine gun on CHAPEAU. one round on exact spot. Request of 14th Inf Bde.
10.20PM	37	4 HE	.461 } to stop trench mortar. Request of 14th Inf. Bde
11.15PM	37	4 HE	.461 }

B/

Time	Bty	no of rounds fired	Target
9.25am	LFG	7	trench 25
9.30am			Bois de VAUX
9.45am	LFG		MARICOURT. Wood from direction of HARDICOURT.
10.15am	LFG	15	S of MARICOURT wood
12.4PM	LFG		PERONNE Rd
1.19PM		14	trench 14. and BOIS de VAUX
2.00PM			31 trench
3.0PM	light HE	50	near 119 Bty position. about 50% were blind.

[illegible] Lt
A/Adjt [illegible]

A. Daily Report. 3/10/15.

Time	Bty	No. of rounds fired	TARGET.
7.50PM	119	45	Point 489. At request 14th Inf. Bde. Enemy believed heard unloading wagons.

B.

			nil

Daily Report. 4/10/15.

A.

Time	Bty.	No. of rounds fired	TARGET.
3.0pm	119	6.	pt 481. enemy shelling trench 15
3.0pm	37	2 HE	pt 481. enemy shelling trench No 15.
3.10pm	37	4 HE.	pt 487. enemy trench mortar on our trenches.
3.45PM	A/115	15	Registering pts in area
1.30PM	B/115	6	Registering pts in area
3 PM	C/115	25	Registering pts in area.
3.30PM	D/115	19	Registering pts in area.

B.

.15PM			Wood in M 9/6 from direction of Q 26 7/5
.45PM			No 15 trench.
.30PM	4.2. HE		MARICOURT WOOD

[illegible] Capt
Adjt Rt group

Daily Report 5/10/15.

A.

Time &c.	Bty.	No. of rounds fired	TARGET.
11.5 am	124	1	Could not be unloaded.
~~[illegible]~~ 11am to 4 PM	~~[illegible]~~ A/115	31	Registration. 415, Q3 1/8, 417. 412, Q2 6/4,
12.30pm to 2.45am	B/115	11	Registration. 434, 439,
10.30AM	C/115	14	Registration. 473, 475, 481, 400x E of 481.
12 pm to 3.30pm	D/115	37	Registration. 464, Q16 4/2

B.

Nil

[illegible] Lieut
adjt [illegible] group

Daily Report 6/10/15

A.

Time	Bty	No. of rounds fired	TARGET
10.20am	A/115	10	Registering. Q 3 1/7; Q 2 6/4.
12 noon	B/115	18	Registering. pt 448, pt 439, Bois FAVIERE.
3.15 PM	B/115	1	test pt 448. 55 secs.
11.50am	C/115	10	Registering. pt 445, pt 481
11 am	D/115	16	Registering.

B.

Nil

[illegible] Lt
Adjt Rt Group.

Daily Report. 7/10/15

A.

Time	Bty	No. of rounds fired	TARGET
3.35 pm	A/115	13	Q 2 9/3
3.40 pm	A/115	11	Q 2 9/3½
1 PM	B/115	23	Registration.
3.30 pm	C/115	8	Registration.
8.5 PM	37	3 HE	Trench mortar. on pt 475. Retaliation.
9.15 PM	37	9 HE (3 blind)	CHAPEAU. at request of 14th Inf Bde. Retaliation.
9.50 PM	37	2 HE	O/B Trench 13 request of infantry.

B.

Time	Bty	No. of rounds fired	TARGET
10.30 am		34	PERONNE. ROAD

[illegible] Lt Col
Cmdg 1st Gp

Daily Report 8-10-1915

A.

Time	Bty.	No. of rounds fired	TARGET
9.30PM	A/115	1	Test by O.C. group. 57 secs
9.30AM	B/115	1	Test by O.C. group 4 mins.
3.30pm	C/115	7	Sap. north of pt A23d 2/0. Retaliation. German snipers
5.0pm	C/115	8	Snipers post pt A10a 1/5 Retaliation. German snipers.
9.30pm	C/115	1	Test by O.C. group. 3 mins.
9.30PM	D/115	1	Test by O.C. group 7 mins.
10.45PM	37	3 HE	Trench mortar opp: trench 27. Request of Infantry.

B.

Daily Report. 1/1/15

A.

Time	Bty.	No. of rounds fired	TARGET
11 am 16 12.30 PM	B/115	10	A 17 a S/O.

B.

Nil

[illegible] Lt
Adjt. Art. Group.

Daily Report. 10/10/15

A.

Time	Btty.	No. of rounds fired	TARGET.
1.10 P.M	C/115	6 rounds	Tr. ~~[illegible]~~ Trench at A23b 1/7

B.

Nil.

[illegible] Capt [illegible]

A.

Daily Report. 11 10/15

Time	Bty.	No. of rounds fired	TARGET.
3PM	120 (A/115)	5	A 9 b 4/5. Working party.
3.30PM	119 (D/115)	4	A 29 d 8/7. Working party.
4.0PM	"	6	A 29 d 7/9. Working party.
4PM	119	4	A 29 d 8/8. Working party.

B.

ML

Daily Report. 12/10/15.

A.

Time	Btty	No. of rounds fired	TARGET.
11·25am	120 (A/115)	8 S 2 HE	In front of trench 29. Retaliation.
10 55am	123 (B/115)	6	N. end of BOIS FAVIERE. Retaliation.
3·45pm	124 (C/115)	10	In front of trench 28. Retaliation.
4PM	119	9 S 6 HE	A 29 d. 7/8.
4·40pm	37	13 S	BOIS FAVIERE. A 17 [illegible] 5/8. Retaliation

B.

Time	Btty	No. of rounds fired	TARGET.
11·20am	LFG.		Trenches 28 and 29.
10 55am	LFG	12	N. end of MARICOURT. Wood.
3·30pm	LFG	6	MARICOURT Wood
4·30am	LFG		MARICOURT Wood.

[illegible] Lt
Adjt RA group

Daily Report. 13/10/15.

A.

Time	Btty.	No. of rounds fired	TARGET.
12.45PM	C/115 (124th)	10	A 23 ~~b~~ b 1/5. Snipers (and rifle grenades) Retaliation.
4.5PM	do	10S 1HE	~~Machine gun emplacement~~ observing Station. A17d 1/6.
5.20PM	37	7S	Working parties. A30a 3/3, A30a 3/7

B.

Nil

[illegible]
Lt Col [illegible] RA group

Daily Report. 14 10/15

A

Time	Bty.	No. of rounds fired	TARGET
9.20 PM	A/115 (120)	1	Test by O.P. 115 Bde. 1 min 10 secs.
3.0 PM	B/115 (123. Bty)	6	BOIS. FAVIERE. Retaliation.
9.19 PM	B/115 (123 Bty)	1	Test. by O.P. 115th Bde. 3 mins 50 secs
9.15 PM	C/115 (124. Bty)	1	Test by O.P. 115th Bde. Opp. trench 16. 50 secs
9.35 PM	D/115 (119. Bty)	1	Test by O.P. 115th Bde. 1 min 30 secs.
12.1 PM	119th Bty	20. S 14. HE	German work. A 29d 7/8
9.50 PM ~~9.15 PM~~ 10 12.40 PM	119th Bty ~~119 Bty~~	5s ~~[illegible]~~	A 29d 7/8. at irregular intervals. ~~do~~
2.15 PM	37	7	T25a 5/0. Working party dispersed.
2 30 am	37	5	Working party. Edge of BOIS. FAVIERE
B			
2.45 PM	LFG	10	BOIS. MARICOURT. from direction of ~~[illegible]~~ HARDECOURT

[illegible] Lt
Adjt RA. group

A. Daily Report. 15/10/15

Time	Bty	No. of Rounds fired	TARGET.
2.25 PM	A/115 (120)	6	A 10 d 3/6.
1.15 PM	B/115 (123)	10	A 17 a 2/7. Machine gun, emplacement
11-30 to 12.30 pm	C/115 (124)	11 S 2H 10 HE	A 23 a 8/2 Machine gun emplacement.
1.3 pm	"	5	A 23 b 2/4. Working party.
3.45 PM	D/115 (119)	7	A 29 d 6/8. German work.
4.20 PM	"	3	A 30 a 1/4.
4.30 PM	37	4	B 8 a 9/9. Working party.
B.			
3 PM	LFG		PERONNE (A23a) from direction of MAUREPAS.

[illegible] adjt RT group.

Daily Report. 16/7/15

A

Time	Bty	No. of rounds fired	TARGET
8.7PM	A/115 (120)	6	BOIS ALLEMAND. ~~[illegible]~~
7.30PM ~~[illegible]~~	B/115 (123)	~~5~~1	~~Making parapet [illegible]~~ A17d 1/6. Red Rocket
10.15PM	C/115 (124)	1S 2HE }	A23b 1/2. Retaliation. Germans bombing our trenches
8.20PM	D/115 (119)	1	A29d 6/8. Red Rocket

B.

Time	Bty	No. of rounds fired	TARGET
7.10PM ~~[illegible]~~		8	Trench 31 from direction of BOIS des TRONES.

[illegible] Lt
Adjt [illegible] Group

Daily Report. 17/10/15.

A.

Time	Bty	No. of rounds fired	TARGET.
5.18 pm	A/115 (120)	6	German trenches A 10 d. Retaliation. Infantry report good result.
1.20 PM	C/115 (124)	2 HE, 2 S } ([illegible])	A. 23. centre. Working party.
12.35 PM	D/115 (119)	6	A 29 d 7/9. Working party.
9.30 pm	119	7	A 29 d 8/7. Enemy grenading our trenches.
11.25 pm	119	4	A 29 d 8/7. at request of Infantry
3.15 PM	37	12	A 24 a 5/8. Working parties.
3.40 PM	37	5	N of MAUREPAS. Working party.
B. 3 PM	LFG	5	Bois de MARICOURT
5 PM	light AE	4	29 trench. [illegible] from direction of GUILLEMONT,

[illegible] Lt
adjt R[illegible] group.

Daily Report. 18 10/15.

A

Time	Bty.	No. of rounds fired	TARGET
1.45 pm	A/114	10	Registering.
12.10 PM	B/114	14	Registering.
3.30 pm	C/114	9	Registering.
3.30 pm	D/114	12	Registering.
11.35 am	37	4	A18c 2/2. Working party.
7.0 am	37	5	Top of CHAPEAU A29d.
B.			
10.15 am	HE	2	Trench 13.
10.30 am	LFG	2	Trench 13
10.30 am	LFG	~~8~~ 12	MARICOURT wood from direction of A24a 9/8
4.25 PM	LFG	4	MARICOURT wood from direction of HARDICOURT.

W J Odlum [illegible]
adjt. RF. Group

Daily Report 19 10/15

A.

Time	Bty.	No. of rounds fired	TARGET.
11·40am	A/114	13	Registering.
3·55PM	A/114	4S	opposite 31 trench. Retaliation.
9·5PM	B/114	7	opposite 25 trench. ~~Retaliation~~ Working party.
12·1PM	B/114	6	Registration.
12·15PM	C/114	4	wood in A24a 5/8. Retaliation.
12·15PM	C/114	~~7~~ ~~6~~ 12	Registration
1·15PM	C/114	4	A23a 6/2 Retaliation.
10am	D/114	21	Registration.
12·1PM	C/117	10	Registration.
11·15AM	119	6	(Wood in) A24b 1/5 Retaliation.
11·0 AM	119	6	A29d 0/8. Retaliation
1·20PM	119	5	A29d 0/8. Retaliation.
3·55PM	120	2. HE	~~for~~ opposite 31 trench. Retaliation. (see A/114)

B.

Time	Bty.	No. of rounds fired	TARGET.
10·15	LFG	8	Trench 18.
10·30AM	LFG. HE.	12 (3 blind)	Trenches No 10 and 11. From direction of B20a.
11·0AM	LFG and 4·2 HE	10	Trenches on PERONNE Rd. reported by 14th Inf. Bde.
11·45AM	LFG		BOIS de MARICOURT
1PM	4·2 HE	10 (3 blind)	A23c, A22d
1·10PM	LFG	3	FROLE NVAUX

W. [illegible]
Adjt. Right Group.

Daily Report. 20 10/15.

A.

Time	Bty.	No. of rounds fired	TARGET.
12.20PM	A/114	8	Registering
4.15PM	B/114	3	A.17a 7/8. Registering zone on left.
4.45PM	B/114	1	A.23b 7/4 Registering zone on right.
3.0PM	C/117	10.	A.17a 9/5, A11c 0/0. Registering.
2.20PM	119	6	B25d 8/7. Working party. Effective.
4.15PM	123	3 HE	A.17a 7/6. Retaliation.

B.

Time	Bty.	No. of rounds fired	TARGET.
12.40PM.	LFG	9	No 19. trench from direction of BOIS d'en HAUT.
2.55PM	LFG	6	No.14. trench
3.50PM			Wood. A15b 4/9.
4.0PM	LFG		No 28 trench. from direction of A24a 4/7
4.0PM	LFG		No 26. trench from direction of BOIS FAVIERE. (Short range)

W. J. [illegible]
Capt RA Grp.

Daily Report. 21 10/15

A.

Time	Bty.	No. of rounds fired	TARGET.
8.45PM	A/114	1	Test No 34. 55 secs.
5.5PM	B/114	1	A 10d 0/3.
6.5PM	B/114	2	A 17a 6/1. Retaliation
8.36PM	B/114	1	Test No 26. 2 mins. 30 secs.
3.45PM	C/114	7	A 24a 5/7. [illegible]
9.16PM	C/114	1	Test No 17. 35 secs.
3.30PM	D/114	6	German trenches. A 29d 7/7.
1.55PM	119	1	A 29d 7/8. (At request of Inspector of Ordnance.
6.5PM	123	2 HE	A 17a 6/1. Retaliation. (see B/114)

B.

3.30PM	4.2.	2	BOIS DE MARICOURT. from north of HARDECOURT.
6.15PM	L.F.G.	6	No 28 trench.

[illegible] Lt.
Adjt. RA. Group.

Daily Report. 22/10/15.

A.

Time	Bty	No. of rounds fired	TARGET.
3.15PM	A/114	8	A11c 3/3.
3.35pm	A/114	6	BOIS FAVIERE. Retaliation.
3.30pm	B/114	4	A17a 8/7
4PM	B/114	4	German O.P., A17c 7/9.
2.30PM	C/114	1	Wood X, A24a 5/7. Retalliation.
3.0PM	C/114	4 }	Barrier A23a 8/2.
3.0PM	C/114	5 HE } (124 Bty)	
9.40PM	C/114	4	Y wood A23d 1/2. at request of E. Surreys.
2.0PM	D/114	8	Working party. A29d 8/9.
3.30PM	D/114	6	A29d 6/8. Retalliation.
B.			
3PM	LFG	5	No 12. trench from direction of HEM.
3.15PM			BOIS MARICOURT.
3.30PM	LFG		No 28 support from direction of A24a 5/7.

Daily Report [illegible]

A.

Time.	Battery	No. of rounds fired	TARGET
12.5 PM	B/114	4	A17a 7/0. Retaliation.
11 AM	C/117	4	Ferme ROUGE. Retaliation.
12.20PM	C/117	14	Registering A4 sector.
3.20PM	C/117	2	B14b 0/9. Working party.
8.40PM	119	3 S 3 HE	Chapeau. at request of E Surreys. Retaliation.

B.

Time.	Battery	No. of rounds fired	TARGET
10 AM 10.55AM	4.2	8	A22b 8/2 from direction of A24b Maricourt wood.
11.50AM			27 Support trench.
12.2 PM	4.2		MARICOURT Wood
12.14PM	4.2	4	Cemetery G8a 4/3 from direction of A33c 5/2
1.15PM	LFG	5	A22b from direction of A30.
3.52PM	LFG		27 and 28 trenches from N edge BOIS FAVIÈRE
8.25PM			MOULIN de FARGNY.

[illegible] Allen [illegible]
Capt RA Group

Daily Report 24/10/15

A

Time	Bty.	No. of rounds fired	TARGET
3·30 PM	A/114	1 S 5 HE (120 Bty)	Opposite 28 trench. German trench mortar on 28 trench.
11·30 PM	A/114	1 S 2 HE (120)	~~A10d 4/3~~ A10d 4/3. Retaliation. French mortar.
7·30 am	B/114	4	Machine gun emplacement. A17a 8/1.
12 30 pm	D/114	2	Chapeau. Retaliation.
2 PM	C/117	9 S	A 2 and A 3 Sectors. Registration.
9·45 am	119	18	Southern end of Y wood. A23d 7/0. (single gun)
~~[illegible]~~	~~119~~	~~[illegible]~~ ~~8 HE~~	~~Chapeau.~~
12·7 PM	119	2	Chapeau. Retaliation.
B.			
9·35 am	4 2	4	A23C, A23a
10·30 am	LFG	8	do
12 7 PM		2	MOULIN de FARGNY.
3 40 PM	LFG		MARICOURT WOOD from direction of BOIS FAVIERE.
4 6 PM	LFG	7	A23a. from direction of BOIS d'en HAUT

[illegible] Lt

adjt [illegible] group.

Daily Report 26 10/15

A

Time.	Batty.	No. of rounds fired	TARGET.
3.0 pm	A/114	6	BOIS FAVIERE. Retaliation.
4.0 pm	A/114	4	do
4.3 pm	A/114	6	do
11.45 am	B/114	4	opposite No 23 trench. Retaliation.
12.30 PM	B/114	4	A 17 a 7/8. Retaliation.
11.4 am	C/117.	8 8	N and S. end of Y. wood. Registration.
11. am	119	15. HE	~~[illegible]~~ A 22 d 4/8
12.45 PM	119	1. HE	Working party A 22 d 7/6

B.

11.43 am	4.2 HE	2	Trenches 23 and 24.
12.12 PM	4.2. HE	2	~~Bois~~ A 22 d.
1.0 PM	LFG	4	A 22 d
1.45 PM			Bois de MARICOURT.
2.25 PM	4.2	3	A 22 b 1/5. From direction of B13.
3.45 PM			Trenches 23 and 24. From direction of A 26 b
3.45 PM		3	MARICOURT. village. — do —
4.06 PM		12	BOIS de MARICOURT. — do —

[signature]
[illegible] RA Group

Daily Report 26/10/15

A.

Time	Bty	No. of rounds fired	TARGET
4·20PM	B/114	10	opposite trenches 26 and 27.
7·15PM	C/114	1	opposite trench 18.
4·20PM	119	4	Southern edge of Y wood. Registering.

B.

Time	Bty	No. of rounds fired	TARGET
4·0PM			MARICOURT. WOOD.

[illegible] Lt
Adjt [illegible]

Daily Report. 27/10/15

Time	Bty	No. of rounds fired	TARGET
11. am	A/114	3	A 10 c 3/6. Working party.
11·20 am	A/114	2 HE (?)	do
3·45 PM	A/114	6	BOIS [illegible] HAUT. Retaliation.
10·30 am	B/114	6	opposite No 26 and 27 trenches. Retaliation
4·30 PM	B/114	6	– do –
5·0 PM	C/114	4	Wood X. A 22 a 2/7. Registration.
9·30 pm to 1 pm	C/114	12	HARDECOURT. Str.
3·15 PM	D/114	12	Woods. H1b, H2ac. Hostile guns.
8 to 12 pm	D/114	12	Southern edge of Y wood.
12 to 2 PM	C/117	20 HE } 3 S }	Y wood.
4·30 PM	C/117	3	A2. sub sector. Registering.
10·45 am	119	2	Trench A 29 d 7/7. Retaliation.
1 PM & 3·45 PM	119	32	Y wood. ~~[illegible]~~
B. 9·30 am	LFG	3	A 23 a 2/7
10·1 am	LFG	17	Trench 23 and BOIS de MARICOURT from direction of A.
10·35 am	LFG	2	MOULIN de FARGNY. from direction of H1.
12·0 PM	4·2	5	MARICOURT – SUZANNE Rd.
3·40 PM		4	No 27 trench

[illegible]
a/g Rt Grp.

Daily Report. 28/10/15.

A.

Time.	Bty.	No. of rounds fired	TARGET.
11.15 AM	A/114	4	A 10 c 3/6. Working party.
4.15 PM	A/114	6 S 15 HE }	German work. A 10 d 6/3.
12.45 PM	A/114	6 S 3 HE }	A 10 d 1/2. Ratcleeter. Germans rifle-grenading our trenches.
	B/114		
11.30 AM	C/114	4	A 23 d 1/1
4.45 PM	C/114	7	A 23 c 9/7.
4.30 PM	C/114	4	A 24 a 4/7. X wood.
	~~[illegible]~~	~~4~~	~~[illegible]~~
4.15 PM	D/114	15	opposite trenches 15 and 16
12.10 PM	C/117	6	A 17 d 0/6. Registering.
12.20 PM	C/117	2	CHAPEAU. Registering.
4.30 PM	C/117	4 HE	Southern edge of Y wood.
B. 1.50 PM	LFG	1	German trenches on CHAPEAU.
4.3 PM	LFG	10	No 27 trench.
4.10 PM	HE	4	BOIS MARICOURT

[illegible] A
[illegible] RA grp

Daily Report. 29/10/15

A.

Time	Bty.	No. of rounds fired	TARGET.
11.35 AM	A/114	3 S 7 HE (100?)	BRICKERY.
1 PM	A/114	6	opposite No 30 Trench Retaliation.
4.45 PM	A/114	10	31 . Retaliation
4.30 PM	A/114	6	BOIS FAVIERE. Retaliation.
11.30 AM	B/114	12	A 17a 7/0. Retaliation.
4.15 PM	B/114	5	BOIS FAVIERE. Retaliation.
11.30 AM	C/114	10 S 14 HE (124)	A 23 a 6/2.
3.30 PM	D/114	8	A 30 b 9/6. Retaliation.
12 noon	C/117	20 HE	Southern edge of Y. wood.

B.

11.20 AM	L F G	12	No 33 support trench. From direction of X wood.
12.30 PM	4 2	6	BOIS. MARICOURT.
1.15 PM	L F G	14	No 34 support trench. From direction of BOIS FAVIERE
4.15 PM	[illegible] HE	11	35 and 36 trench. From direction of Bois Faviere.

[illegible] 16
[illegible] group

Daily Report: 30/10/15

A.

Time	Bty.	No. of rounds fired	TARGET
1.28PM	A/114	6	Opposite trench No 30. Retaliation.
4.0PM	A/114	2 S 8 HE	Brickery A 4 b 3/3.
4.45PM	A/114	12 S 6 HE	Wood A 10 a 5/3.
6.43PM	A/114	3 S 3 HE	Opposite No 30. Retaliation for rifle grenades
7.33PM	A/114	9	- - - do - - - -
10 AM	B/114	5	A 17 d 0/6. German O.P.
3.45PM	B/114	6	Opposite No 26 and 26. Retaliation.
3.15PM	C/114	10 S 12 HE	~~Y wood~~ German works between Y wood and PERONNE Rd
12.30PM	D/114	8	Y wood.
2.15PM	D/114	18	B 26 d 8/4
2.45PM	D/114	10	Y wood.
4.45PM	D/114	6	Y wood. Southern edge.
3.30PM	D/114	12	Y wood.
11.30am	~~37~~ C/117	9 S 4 HE	A 10 c 8/3.
2.15PM	C/117	4	Mounted party of Germans A 6 d 4/3.
11.35am	119	6 HE	Chapeau. Retaliation.
4.40PM	119	26 S 25 HE	Y wood.
B.			
11.20am	HE	5	MOULIN de FARGNY from direction BOIS. HEM.
12.30PM		7	BOIS de VAUX from BOIS de HEM.
1.23PM			MARICOURT. WOOD
3.32PM	HE		No 27 support
3.45PM	HE	16	No 18 support
7.5PM		8	No 14 trench.

[illegible] Lt
a/Adj RA Group

Daily Report. 31st Oct.

A.

Time.	Bty.	No. of rounds fired	TARGET.
10.40AM	A/114	12	Wood in A10a. Retaliation.
10.50AM	A/114	6	A.16d 2/4. Retaliation.
2.7PM	A/114	12	opposite No 31 trench. Retaliation.
2.7PM	A/114	12	" " 28 "
3.25PM	C/114	5	Wood x. A29a. Retaliation.
~~[illegible]~~	~~[illegible]~~	~~[illegible]~~	~~[illegible] ([illegible]) [illegible]~~
11.55AM	37	8	A17a 8/6. Working party. effective.
12.35PM	37	4 HE 2 S	A18a 3/3. Working party. effective.
2.45PM	37 ~~[illegible]~~ [illegible]	20 HE 1 S	MAUREPAS
3.30PM	37	2 HE	Bois de FAVIERE.

B.

Time.	Bty.	No. of rounds fired	TARGET.
8.20AM		2	No 10 trench.
10.40 AM	LFG		No 29 and 30 trenches.
11.0AM	4.2. How	8	SUZANNE.
2.38PM	LFG	24	A23a 5/5.

[illegible] Lieut RA
Adjt RA group

21st Division

97th Bde: R.F.A.
Vol: 3

121/7761

Nov. 15.

3e
3.

Appendix to W.D. for
Nov. 1915

Details of Firing
97th Bde R.F.A.

Eq

3rd
Ew

IX

Army Form C. 2118.

Instructions regarding War Diaries and Intelligence Summaries are contained in F. S. Regs., Part II. and the Staff Manual respectively. Title pages will be prepared in manuscript.

WAR DIARY
or
INTELLIGENCE SUMMARY.
(Erase heading not required.)

Place	Date	Hour	Summary of Events and Information	Remarks and references to Appendices
ARMENTIERES	1915		Brigade Ammunition retired to NIEPPE STATION	
	Nov. 1		D Bty. arrived from HAZEBROUCK + took up position in action at C 19 b 6½ 6½ (C 36 N W)	C 36 N W
	" 2		2/Lt. Caslon attached 'C'. 2/Lt Brunton from 'C' to B A C	
	" 9		Lieut Dunlay joined from Home and posted to B A C. Lieut Martin attached to 'B'	
	" 12		The Brigade took part in the bombardment of FORT SENARMONT Ammunition Expended 454 H.E.	
	" 18		Brigade inspected by General Franks. Major Belcher posted to 53 Brigade R F A (To Command)	
	" 19		Captain O'Malley joined and posted to Command 'A' Bty.	
	" 23		D/97 attached to 95 Bde RA for tactical purposes.	
	" 24		Brigade having no longer tactical command Headquarters vacated. Lt Col Pottinger, organized Flash Spotting stations for Second Army for this purpose took up new quarters at 83 Rue Sadi Carnot. Two F.S. stations installed.	
	" 25		2/Lt Hermann joined from Base + attached to D/97. 2/Lieut T. W. Caslon killed in action. 2/Lieut Amoroso posted from 'B' to 'C'/97	
	" 27		Lieut Bracecamps joined from Base + posted to B/97	
	" 30		Brigade still in Armentieres. Batteries distributed as under for tactical purposes.	
			A/97 attached 95 Bde RA In position C 20 d 8.8 C/97 attached 96 Bde RA In position I 9 c 5.9	
			B/97 " 94 " " " C 26 b 9.9 D/97 -do- 95 -do- " C 19 b 6½ 6½	
			Cecil Pottinger for Lt Col R F A	MAP Reference

2353 Wt. W2544/1454 700,000 5/15 D. D. & L. A.D.S.S./Forms/C. 2118.

Comdg 97 B

NOVEMBER.
1915

Daily Report. 1/11/15.

A

Time	Bty	No. of rounds fired	TARGET.
10.30 a.m	119	6	Working party. Chapeau de Gendarme.
10.30 a.m	124	20	Verifying registration.
10.30 a.m	37	9	Working party, Chapeau de Gendarme
10.30 a.m	37	4	" " , A1 b 53.
10.30 a.m.	120.	10	Verifying registration, A9 b 9.2 + A10 c 2
10.30 a.m	123	20	Verifying registration.
11.55 a.m.	37	3	Bois de Favière.
2.55 p.m.	120	6	Registration A10c + A10d.
4 p.m	124	5	Retaliation, trenches opposite Perrone Rd.

B.

Time	Bty	No. of rounds fired	TARGET.
9.50 a.m	Light field gun	3	Perrone Road.
10 a.m.	" "	2	Road A 22 c.
10.20 a.m.	" "	3	" "
3.30 p.m	4.2 c How	3	Maricourt Wood.
3.45 p.m.	light field gun	4	S side Perrone Wood.

T. J.O'Brien Lt. R.F.A.
for Adjt. Rt. Group Art.

Daily Report 2/11/15

A.

Time	Bty.	No. of rounds fired	TARGET
1.5 P.M.	37 Sectn	4 H.E.	Retaliation. Listening Post Chapeau de Gendarme
7.10 P.M.	37 Bty	{6 shrapnel {4 H.E.	B13 b 5.5 Maurepas Station.
12.35 p.m	119.	6 shrap.	Retaliation. Listening Post Chapeau de Gendarme
2 P.M.	119	6 H.E.	" " " "
10.30 P.M.	119	6 shrapnel	Y Wood.
7.10 P.M	124	6 shrapnel	B13 b 5.5. Maurepas Station.

B.

10.15 am		6 H.E.	Moulin de Fargny from direction of HEM. WOOD
12.30 P.M.	LFG	3	Moulin de Fargny.
12.35 P.M.	LFG		A 23, a Peronne Road.
1.40 P.M.	Possible 5.9 cm.	6 H.E.	Moulin de Fargny from direction of HEM WOOD.
~~1.45 P.M.~~	~~L.F.G.~~	~~3~~	

for Adjt. RA T. H. Brown Lt.

Daily Report 3/11/15.

A/

Time	Bty.	No. of rounds fired	TARGET.
1.45 P.M	37	4 S.	Working party, road A 30. d 3.9.
4.53 P.M.	119	{5 S {3 H.E.	Y Wood.
5.56 P.M.	119	{2 S. {5 H.E.	Retaliation. Listening Post. Chapeau de Gendar
B.			
5.12 P.M.		3 H.E.	Moulin de Fargny.

T. J. O'Brien Lt
for Adjt. Right Group Arty.

Daily Report 4/11/15

A.

Time Fd.	Bty.	No. of rounds fired	TARGET.
12.20 P.M.	37 Sect	4 H.E.	~~Retaliation~~ B 25 d 3.8. Party on Road.
1.10 P.M.	37	4 H.E.	Retaliation at request Infantry. Chapeau de Gendar
8.45 P.M.	37 Sect	6 H.E.	Retaliation. Y wood.
119.12.10 P.M.	119	3 S. 4 H.E.	Retaliation. Chapeau de Gendarme.
3.30 P.M.	119	6 S.	Verifying Zones.
5.5 P.M.	119	10 H.E.	Retaliation; Chapeau de Gendarme.
9.10 P.M.	119	25 S.	Ferme Rouge.
10.40 A.M.	120x	60 S	Wire in front Y wood.
1.10 P.M.	120	4 H.E. 6 S	Retaliation at request Infantry A 10 d 6.2.
B. 10.10 A.M.	L.F.G.		18 S. Trench from direction Maurepas.
10.30 A.M.	4.2 How.	15	16 + 17 trench from about 1,200x S of Maurepa
11.5 A.M.	L.F.G.	4	From direction Curlu, on Maricourt Wood.
11.40 A.M.	4.2 How.		13, 14 + 15 trenches.
11.50 A.M.	L.F.G.	3	20 S. trench direction Maurepas.
1.30 P.M.	4.2 How.		Between lines W. of Y Wood.
12.40 P.M.	L.F.G.	8 H.E.	Maricourt Wood + No 28 trench from dir B. de Favière
3 P.M.	L.F.G.	5	About 1000x S of Maurepas.
3.35 P.M.	L.F.G.	5	Maricourt Wood, (3 blind.)
4.20 P.M.	L.F.G.	3	20 S. trench.
9.5 P.M.		5 Salvos	About 15 trench.

T. J. O'Brien. Lt.
for Adjt. R.A. Group.

Daily Report 5/11/15

A.

Time	Bty	No. of rounds fired	TARGET
10.30 AM	37 X	3 H.E	Retaliation. Trench at foot of Chapeau
11.45 AM	37	4 H.E	Verification of Register. A 23 d 10.
11.45 AM	37 X	4 H.E.	
12.30 P.M	37	1 H.E.	Farm A.6 b 11.
8.5 P.M	37 X	4 H.E.	Southern corner Y Wood. Request of Infant
10.15 AM	119	2 H.E.	Retaliation. Tr. at foot of Chapeau.
10.40 AM	119	4 H.E.	Retaliation. Y Wood.
8.20 P.M	119	6 H.E.	Y Wood.
11.33 AM.	120	17 S	Retaliation. Opposite 30 + 31 Trenches.
10.30 P.M	120	4 S	Working party. A 15 b 9.8
11.30 AM	123	6 S	A 17 c 8 9
3.40 P.M	123	12 S	A 17 a 1.8.
3.45 P.M.	123	6 H.E	A 17 c 2.4.
9.130–11.20 A.M.	124	20 S	Trench and wire A 23 C 9.9.
8.15 P.M	124	6 S	Opposite 17 + 18 Trenches.

B.

Time	Bty	No. of rounds fired	TARGET
10.10 A.M.	4.2 How	4	Maricourt Wood S.E. edge. Also 17 Trench
10.30 A.M.		6 H.E.	Moulin de Fargny from direction Hem W.
11.10 A.M.		2	Parapet 18 Trench.
11 A.M.		2	On their barrier Perrone Road.
11.15 AM.	L.F.G.		Our trenches crossing Perrone Road.
11.45 AM.	L.F.G.	2	Maricourt Wood

T. J. O'Br...

Daily Report. 6/11/15

A

Time	Bty.	No. of rounds fired	TARGET.
3.15 P.M	37	2 H.E	Re-registered Pt. A 11 C 0.0.
4.20 P.M	37 X	2 H.E.	Retaliation on Chapeau, at request of Infantry.
2.30 P.M	119	12 S.	Verification of register Wood H 2 a 3.7
3.45 P.M	119	6 S	Retaliation trench foot of Chapeau.
1 P.M	120	13 S 5 H.E.	Retaliation.
2.30 P.M.	120	19 S	Verification of Register pts. A 10 d 5.3, A 10 d 6.2, A 10 c 5.5, A 10 d 0.3
3.30 P.M.	120	12 S	Retaliation opposite 31 trench.
11.30 AM	123	6 H.E	A 17 c 8.9
12.45 P.M.	123	4 S 4 H.E	Working party A 17 a 9.4.
1.30 P.M	123	20 S	Registering.
11.30 a.m	124	7 S	A 17 d 2.6 to A 23 d 2.7
12.30 – 1 P.M	124	12 S	Verification of Register Y Wood, N.E corner in particular
B.			
1.30 P.M.	L.F.G	2	Vaux Wood.
3.40 P.M to 3.55 P.M		8 H.E.	Nos. 12, 14 and 15 trench from direction Bois de Hem.
4 P.M.		2	Vaux Wood.

T. J. O'Brien Lt.
for Adjutant
P.V. Group Arty

Daily Report 7/10

A.

Time	Bty	No of rounds fired	TARGET
9.40 AM	119	4 H.E.	Retaliation, trench at foot of Chapeau
10. P.M.	119	5 S.	Retaliation. Wood B 26 d 5/3.

B.

10.45 AM.	Air Crash Gun	4 gun	battery from direction of Maurepas.
12.25 P.M.	L.F.G.	1	On communication trench along Peronne Road. A 22 b 8.2.
9.30 P.M.	About 4		Moulin de Fargny from direction Mauripas.

T. J. O'Brien Lt
for Adjt. Rt. Group

Daily Report. 8/11/15

A

Time	Bty.	No. of rounds fired	TARGET.
11·50AM	37	8 H.E.	Hardicourt ~~Maure~~pas Station. A 18 b 5.4 ~~B 12 b 55.5~~
2·10 P.M	37	2 H.E	Retaliation, Chapeau de Gendarme
1·30 P.M.	37	2 H.E.	Verifying range.
2·10 P.M.	37	2 H.E.	~~...~~ Top of Chapeau. Request of Infant ~~C.R.A. 5 Div.~~
3·50 P.M.	119	4 S	Trench at foot of Chapeau.
8·30 P.M.	119	16 S / 2 H.E	Retaliation. Y Wood.
3·50 P.M.	120	2 S	Opposite 28 Register.
3·15 P.M.	123	1 S	Test. C.R.A. 5 Div. Arty.
11·30 A.M.	124	10 S. / 14 H.E	Verification pts. A 23 a 8.2, A 23 b 1.3.

B.

Time	Bty.	No. of rounds fired	TARGET.
1 A.M.		5 (13 salvo of 4)	over 19 and 20 Support Trenches from direction of Chapelle de Carlu.
1·40 P.M	L.F.G.	6	Peronne Barrier. from direction of Maricourt.
1·45 P.M	4·2 How.	12	15 Trench from N.E. of Maurepas.

T. J. O'Brien
Lt. for C.O. ... Right Group ...

Daily Report. 9/11/15

A.

Time.	Btz.	No. of rounds fired	TARGET.
~~2.10~~	~~37 X~~	~~2 HE~~	~~Retaliation, Chapeau de Gendarme.~~
4.5 P.M	37	4 H.E.	Machine Gun Emplacement. A23 b 2.4.
7.5 P.M	37	1 H.E.	A 11 C.O.O. Rocket Test.
7.3 P.M	119	1 S	Y wood " "
7.1 P.M	120	8 S	29 trench. " "
10.25 a.m.	123	12 S 2 HE.	Retaliation. Front line opposite 23 Tr.
12.30 a.m	123	20 S	Verification of Registers.
1.20 P.M.	123	10 S	Retaliation. Bois d'en Haut.
7 0 P.	123	3 S	28 trench. Rocket Test.

B.

10 AM.	L.F.C.	30 S	S. W. Corner Maricourt Wood (Replied) bearing M 130° from A23 a 2.7
10.25	LFC	8	23 Support Trench. (Retaliated).
12.30 pm.	LFC	6	Maricourt Wood
2.25 P.M.	LFC	2	No 13 Listening Post.

Daily Report. 10/11/15

A.

Time	Btty.	No. of rounds fired	TARGET.
12.35 P.M.	37	2 H.E	A17d 2.5. Retaliation at request of Infantry.
11.55. AM	119	6 S	Loopholes in Observation Post H1c 6.6.
2.40 P.M.	119	4 H.E.	" " " "
3.50 P.M.	119	2 S	" " "
4.20 P.M.	119	4 S	
11.45 AM.	120	12 S	Verification of Register Mk. A10c 0.7, A10c 3½.7, A10a 5.3.
11.50 am.	120	9 HE.	A9d 9½.7. ~~Verification of Register.~~ [Loop-holes in 2nd line.]
8.20 am.	120	2 S.	~~Retaliation~~ [Small party]. Nr. Bricqueterie.
4.15 P.M	120	8 S	Bois de Favière. Retaliation.
9.40. AM.	123	6 S	Working Party. A11c 2.5.
10.40 AM.	123	6 S	Retaliation, opposite 23 trench.
10.40 AM.	124	11 S	Retaliation A23b 2.9

B.

Time	Btty.	No. of rounds fired	TARGET.
10.30 AM	L.F.a	5 S	On Vaux School from direction of Hem Wood H 7.
10.32 AM	L.F.a	15	Bois de Maricourt over 27 trench from direction. Bois d'en Haut.
10.35 AM.		3 S	Dragoon Wood from direction of Maurepas.
~~6.10 P.M.~~	~~4.2 How~~	~~6~~	
3.52 P.M.	4.2 How	6	
6.10 P.M.	4.2 How	6	Behind 28 Trench.

T. J. O'Brien Lt
for Capt. R. Group Cmdr.

Daily Report 11/10/15

A

Time	Bty.	No. of rounds fired	TARGET.
3·45 PM	37.	6 H.E 3 S.	A 23 d 0·3 — A 23 d 9·0.
9·55 am	119	2 H.E. 2 S	Observation Station. H 1 c 6·6.
11·28 AM	119	4 S	" " "
12·10 PM	119	4 S	" " "
2·30 PM	119	2 S 2 HE.	" " "
2·45 PM.	119	1 S.	" " "
3·45 PM.	120	6 S	Retaliation. Bois de Favière.
12·30 PM	123	5 H.E 5 S	New Work. A 11 c 2·5.
3·25 PM	123	5 H.E. 6 S	Saphead opposite 26 trench.
8·55 AM	124	7 S	Retaliation. Bois d'en Haut.

B.

Time	Bty.	No. of rounds fired	TARGET.
7·45 AM.	L.F.G.	3 Shrap.	N. end of Bois de Maricourt.
8·20 AM	L.F.G.	15 Shrap.	Retaliation Bois de Maricourt. (Replie on B. Favie
11·50 AM.	L.F.G.	3 Shrap.	
3·15 PM		6 Shrap.	Over 17 trench.
4·10 PM.	L.F.G	2 "	Over 17 trench.
4·15 PM	L.F.G	1	Peronne Road. 100x behind trenches.

T. J. O'Brien
for Adjt. R. Group

Daily Report 12/11/15

A

Time	Bty.	No. of rounds fired	TARGET
3.50PM	119	1	Listening Post. CHAPEAU.
7 AM	120	1	A10c 1/6 } Snipers gallery
11 AM	120	11S 10HE }	A10c 1/6
3.30PM	120	16S 5HE }	A4c 1/9 gun emplacements.
11.30am	123	5	A17a 9/4. Snipers.
12.5 PM	123	7S 4HE }	A11c 2/4. new german work.
10.50 am	124	2	A24d. Working party.
11.15 am	124	4	B20a 1/6. Working party.
12.25 AM	124	4	A23a 9/1. Retaliation.
11.45 AM	124	2S 8HE }	A23b 2/7. Sniper's post.
3.20PM	124	6	A23a 9/1. Retaliation.
3.35PM	124	3	Bois-d'en-HAUT. Retaliation.
4.0PM	124	6	Wood in A24a. Retaliation.
12.5 PM	37	4S 8HE }	Dug outs at A30 0/7.

B.

Time	Bty.	No. of rounds fired	TARGET
3 PM	LFG	3	A15b
3.45PM	LFG	15	A16b from direction of A24a.
3.25PM	LFG		MARICOURT. WOOD.

[signature] Lt
adjt Right Group.

Daily Report 13·11·15.

A

Time.	Bty.	No. of rounds fired.	TARGET.
10.30 AM	119	10 S 2 HE	B26d 9/3. Hostile Battery. Retaliation.
12.1 PM	119	5 S 2 HE	A29d 4/8. Retaliation (for MOULIN.)
2·10 PM	120	6	Opposite No 28 trench. Retaliation.
12·5 PM	123	12	A10d 8/3 A11c 2/4 } Retaliation.
9·55 AM	124	3	A23a 9/1. Retaliation.
11·0 AM	124	8	B20a 1/5.
11·40 AM	124	3	BOIS d'en HAUT. Retaliation.
11·55 AM	124	6	do.
12·40 PM	124	6 S 2 HE	A23b 2/3. Retaliation.
3·5 PM	124	4	BOIS d'en HAUT. Retaliation.
3·20 PM	124	6	Opposite No 22 trench. Retaliation.
10·5 AM	37	3 HE	CHAPEAU. Retaliation.

B/

Time.	Bty.	No. of rounds fired.	TARGET.
9·4 AM	LFG	5 HE	BOIS de VAUX.
10 AM	LFG	6 HE	Eastern edge BOIS de VAUX. from direction of BOIS de HEM.
10 AM	4 2	10 HE	Behind No 1? trench.
10·40 AM	6 ins	20 HE	G9c 0/8. from direction S of HEM.
11·35 AM	LFG	9	PERONNE RD. A22b
11·50 AM	LFG.	12	MARICOURT WOOD. No 27 and 28 trenches
11·55 AM	LFG	3 HE	MOULIN de FARGNY.
12.30 PM	LFG	12	MARICOURT. WOOD.
2·0 PM	LFG	6	No 28 trench.
3 5 PM	LFG	6	No 22 trench. from direction S of HARDECOURT.

[illegible]

Daily Report. 14/11/15.

A.

Time	Bty.	No. of rounds fired	TARGET.
12.5 PM	119	1 S } 2 HE }	H.1 c 6/6. House
12.5 PM	119	1	A 30 c 6/6
10.45 AM	120	6	Snipers loop holes A 10 c 8/4.
10.15 PM	120	6 S } 6 HE }	opposite No 35 trench. Retaliation.
B.			
11.15 AM	LFG	5	A 22 b
12.27 PM	LFG	7	No 17 and 18 trenches from direction of B 26
2.25 PM	4.2 How	6	A 22 b
10.10 PM			No 35 trench.

[illegible] Lt
24th RA Group

Daily Report 16 4/15

A.

Time.	Bty	No. of rounds fired.	TARGET
10.30AM	119	10 S 8 HE	H1C 7/3 (8HE); Y wood (10S); CHAPEAU (10S)
6.10 PM	119	8 S 4 HE	FERME ROUGE.
8.20 PM	119	5 HE	Y wood. Retaliation.
11.30 AM	120	11 S 3 HE	Snipers gallery. A10c 3/6.
12.15 PM	120	2	Opposite No 35 trench. German Daeurring.
3.25 PM	120	6 S 3 HE	Opposite No 29 trench. Retaliation.
3.45 PM	120	34 8 S 4 HE	do
4.20 PM	120	8 S 3 HE	BOIS FAVIERE. Retaliation
10.45 AM	123	22 S 10 HE	A17a 9/2.
12.5 PM	123	1	Test by O.P. group.
1.45 PM	123	4	Opposite No 27 trench. Retaliation.
10.0 AM 10.30 AM	124 124	22 S 10 HE	A23c 9/6. Machine gun emplacement Wood A24a and Y wood.
4.5 PM	124	20 6	Bois d'en HAUT. Retaliation.
11.30 AM	37	1 S 14 HE	Trenches A23b 7/7 – A23b 9/9 and A30a 0/6
12.5 PM	37	1 HE	Test by O.P. group.
4.10 PM	37	5 HE	Wood in A10a. Retaliation.

(21)

B.

Time.	Bty	No. of rounds fired.	TARGET
1.35 PM	LFG		No 27 trench
3.45 PM	LFG	15	No 26 and 27 support trenches.
4 PM	42	40	MARICOURT. WOOD and trenches No 29
5.50 PM	LFG	10	No 15 and 16 trenches.
8.15 PM	LFG	12	No 15 trench

[illegible] Lieut.
[illegible] O.P. group

Daily Report. 16/11/15

A.

Time	Bty.	No. of rounds fired	TARGET.
12.40 PM	119	10.	gun position in B 26 d. Retaliation.
1.15 PM	119	4 HE	House in H.1c 7/3
11.35 AM	120	1	To test corrector.
12.15 PM	120	4 S } 5 HE }	A 9 d 7/9. movement in trenches. Result effective.
3.0 PM	120	13 S } 4 HE }	Opposite No 30 trench. Retaliation.
4.5 PM	123	6	A 10 d 8/2. Smoke seen in german trenches.
12.35 PM	124	5	A 23 b 1/1. Retaliation
12.40 PM	124	8	Wood A 24 a. Retaliation.
2.0 PM	124	20 S } 4 HE }	A 17 d 3/7 and PERONNE RD. barricades. Retaliation.
1.0 PM	37	3 HE	A 6 b 1/1. House. One direct hit.
3.40 PM	37	5 HE	A 33 d 0/5.

B.

Time	Bty.	No. of rounds fired	TARGET.
11.43 AM	LFG	~~3~~ 9	No 15 trench ~~from direction [illegible]~~
12.30 PM	4.2	~~6~~ 18	PERONNE Road.
12.33 PM	LFG	~~7~~ 11	BOIS de VAUX. from direction of B26d
2.0 PM	4.2	?	PERONNE Rd from direction of FERME. ROUGE
2.50 pm	LFG	12	No 30 trench. from a direction due EAST.
4.25 PM	4.2 Shrapnel	2	100x in front of 124 Bty

[illegible] 2/Lt
Lieut RA [illegible]

17/Nov/15

Daily Report.

A.

Time	B.G.	No. of rounds fired	TARGET.
11·5 AM	119	12	B 26 d. Retaliation.
7·55 PM	119	12	Y wood. Retaliation
9·35 AM	120	3	To test corrector and range.
9 AM	123	2	A 10 b 9/2. Working party. Effective.
11·5 AM	124	2	A 17 d 2/4. To test corrector and range.
11·40 AM	37	4 HE	CHAPEAU. Retaliation.
7·55 PM	37	5 HE	opposite No 16·17·18 trenches. Retaliation successful.
B.			
10·55 AM	LFG. HE	[illegible] 25	No 13 trench. from direction of B 26
7·5 PM	LFG	8	No 15 trench
7·50 PM			Enemy bombing No 16·17·18 trenches.

[illegible] Lt
adjt RA group

Daily Report 18th

A.

Time	Bty	No. of rounds fired	TARGET
9.55AM	120	2 S 9 HE	Party of Germans on MONTAUBAN – BRIQUETERIE (Rd)
12.25AM	120	4 S 5 HE	A10c 4/5. M.G. emplacement. at request of Q.V.R.
3.55PM	120	4	A16c 3/6. Movement and smoke seen in the trenches.
8.47AM	124	8	A23b 1/2. Retaliation.
9.4AM	124	4	A17d 2/6 – do –
9.10AM	124	2	A23b 4/8 – do –
10.45AM	124	4	A23b 1/2 – do –
1.0PM	124	1	A6c 4/4. Party of Germans (30)
3.30PM	124	10 S 6 HE	~~B~~ PERONNE. Rd. Barricades. Retaliation.
12.55PM	37	1 HE	opposite No12 trench. ~~[illegible]~~ Test.
10.15PM	37	6 HE	opposite No18 trench. Retaliation for enemy bombs. effective.

B.

8.40AM	LFG	12	PERONNE. Rd. From a direction due East.
9.0AM	LFG	~~3~~ 8	No 21 trench. From direction. N of MAUREPAS.
10.50AM	4.2	2	Cross Roads A13d 8/0. From direction S23.
11.0AM	LFG	~~3~~8	No18 trench.
3.0PM	LFG	18	No18 trench. from direction of HEM wood
3.20PM	LFG	8	No19-20. trenches.

Daily Report: 19 4/15.

A

Time.	Bty.	No. of rounds fired.	TARGET.
12.03 ×	119	12	Road B19b 7/2 to B20a 2/6.
×	120	12	MONTAUBAN – BRICKERY. Road
×	123	12	Road A17b 7/6
3.15 PM	123	3	A17b 4/9.
×	124	12	Road A18b 7/0 to 5/5
×	37	7 HE	HARDECOURT. Rly. Stn.

× At irregular intervals during the day

B.

Nil

W.G. Odlum Lieut
Adjt. Rt. Group

Daily Report. 20/4/15

A

Time.	Bty.	No. of rounds fired	TARGET.
3.25PM	120	6	A10D 1/3. Retaliation.
3.55PM	120	8	A10c 2/6. A10d 1/2.
5.55PM	37	4. HE	A10d 8/2. Machine Gun.
B.			
3.15PM	LFG	4	No 28 trench.

[illegible]
[illegible]

Daily Report. 21/4/15

A.

Time.	Bty.	No. of rounds fired.	TARGET.
10·35 AM	119	2 S. – 1 HE	Listening post on CHAPEAU.
3·5 PM	119	12	New trenches on the CHAPEAU and A 29 b
10·38 AM	120	6	opposite No 35 trench. Retaliation.
10·55 AM	120	3 S – 3 HE	do – – –
12·10 PM	120	7 S – 3 HE	opposite No 29 trench.
3·15 PM	120	1	MONTAUBAN. Road. party of germans.
3·39 PM	120	6	S.O.S. sent by O.C group. opposite No 30·31 trenches.
11·50 AM	123	14	A 17 a 5/6. Retaliation.
11·0 AM	124	10 S – 15 HE	A 23 a 1/2 and A 23 b 2/3.
2·35 PM	124	12	BOIS-d'en-HAUT. Retaliation.
11·30 AM	37	10 HE	PERONNE Rd.
1·15 PM	37	3 HE	PERONNE Rd. Retaliation.
12·55 PM	37	5 HE	MONTAUBAN – BRICKERY. Rd.
4·15 PM	37	3 HE	– – – do – – – – –
B.			
10·35 AM	4·2 ~~[illegible]~~	37 (5 Min.)	Wood A 15 a 4/9 from direction of BERNAFAY. wood
10·45 AM		20	No 18 trench. from direction of A 19 b.
11·45 AM	LFG		Nos 22·23·24 trenches.
1·23 PM			Behind 18 trench
1·30 PM	4·2	3	A 16 b.
2·30 PM	LFG	15 [illegible]	MARICOURT Wood from the East. 3 fell on the edge of the village
B			
10·35 AM	4·2	37 (5 Mins)	Wood A 15 a 4/9. From direction of BERNAFAY Wood.
10·45 AM	LFG	20	No 18 trench. From direction of A 19 b.
11·45 AM	LFG	8	22·23·24. trenches.
1·23 PM	LFG	6	Behind No 18 trench.
1·30 PM	4·2	3	A 16 b
2·30 PM	LFG	15	MARICOURT WOOD. 3 shell fell on edge of village. from E direction. ~~of the EAST~~.

[illegible] Report. 22 11/15.

A.

Time.	Bty.	No. of rounds fired	TARGET.
12 noon	119	14 S / 7 HE	CHAPEAU. A29d 0/8 and A29d 8/6.
10.15 PM	119	6	working party on CHAPEAU. Reported by infantry
10.40 AM	120	3	To verify range and corrector.
12.10 PM	120	5 S / ~~9~~HE	A16c 6/4 M. G. emplacement.
10.45 AM	123	10	A17c 3/7. New wire in German trenches.
11.45 AM	123	4 S. 10 HE	Dug outs. A11c 2/1.
11.30 AM	124	7	new trench on CHAPEAU. A29d 8/8 enfilade
12.25 PM	124	4	A26b 0/5. German work.
7.15 PM	124	4	New trench on CHAPEAU.
10.50 AM	37	3 HE	new trench on ~~[illegible]~~ CHAPEAU
11.45 AM	37	8 HE	A2~~9~~d 6/8 to A29d 8/8.
1.40 PM	37	8 HE	A23d 8/0 and A23 (centre). Retaliation
11.20 PM	37	2 HE	A23d 8/0

B.

Time.	Bty.	No. of rounds fired	TARGET.
11.55 AM	LFG	4	MARICOURT WOOD. behind 26 and 27 trenches.
12.5 PM	4.2	~~[illegible]~~ 24	No 15 and 16 trenches. From direction of B.20

[illegible] Lt
Adjt Bt Group.

Daily Report 23/4/15

A.

Time.	Bty.	No. of rounds fired.	TARGET.
1.30 P.M.	117	2 H.E. 2 Shrap	Listening Post Chapeau de Gendarme.
9.0 p.m.	119	2 H.E. 2 Shrap.	Working Party Chapeau de Gendarme
3-45 pm	37	3 H.E.	Trench at South corner of Y wood.

B.

[illegible]

[illegible] RA
for Adj. Rt. Gp.

Daily Report 24/11/15

A.

Time.	Bty.	No. of rounds fired.	TARGET.
3.15 pm.	119	6 shrap.	Listening post on Chapeau de Gendarme
6.5 pm	119	2 shrap.	Listening post on Chapeau de Gendarme
7.45 pm	119	2 shrap.	Listening post on Chapeau de Gendarme
3.0 pm	120	4 shrap.	at A 10 C 2/6
3.45 pm	120	12 shrap.	Bois de Faivère
2.45 pm	123	4 shrap.	working party A 17 A 8/2.
10.53 am.	124	5 shrap.	working party A 23 B 2/4
2.15 pm	124	10 shrap.	~~hostile gun A24 B 1/6~~ wood A 24 A 4/8
3.30 pm	124	10 shrap.	hostile gun in wood A 24 B 1/6
4.30 pm	37	3 H.E.	transport on BOIS DES TRONE – HARDECOURT Road

B.

2.45 pm	light field gun	9	Communication trench A22 B 5/2. True Bearing taken from G4c 9/6 was 63°.
3.20 pm	light field gun	12	Bois de HARICOURT. located in wood A24 B 1/6
6.0 pm		12	B 1 Sub-sector. the shells came from direction of S.E. Corner of BOIS des TRONE

S.T. Bulteel
S.R.A.
for Adj. Rt. Grp.

Daily Report 22 12

A.

Time	Bty.	No. of rounds fired	TARGET.
10.15 a.m.	119	10 HE	HEM, retaliation for enemy shelling SUZANNE
12.15 a.m.	119	4 Shr.	B 25 B 5/4
1.27 pm	119	7 Shr. 6 HE	House H1c 7/6 in retaliation for shelling MOULIN de FAGNY
3.0 pm	119	3 Shr 7 HE	Listening post at foot of Chapeau de Gendarme
3.5 pm	119	5 Shr 5 HE	FERME ROUGE
6.0 pm	119	4 Shr.	New trench and Listening Post on Chapeau
6.45 pm	119	4 Shr.	" " " " " "
7.45 pm	119	4 Shr.	" " " " " " "
8.33 pm	119	1 Shr.	New trench on "Chapeau" "
10.53 am	120	2 Shr.	MONTAUBAN - BRIQUETERIE Road
11.35 am	120	12 Shr 5 HE	BOIS de FAVIÈRE
3.25 pm	120	3 Shr 5 HE	Trench opposite our no 34 trench Retaliation
3.53 pm	120	6 Shr.	Trench opposite our no 29 Trench Retaliation
11.15 am	123	8 Shr.	BOIS de FAVIERE
1.45 pm	123	16 Shr	Wire in front of Y wood
3.35 pm	123	3 HE	BOIS de FAVIERE
10.15 am	124	4 Shr 4 HE	BOIS d'en HAUT
11.10 am	124	4 HE	Wood A24B1/6
1.20 pm	124	4 Shr	Working party
12.30 pm	124	12 Shr	Wood A24A
2.50 pm	124	15 Shr	BOIS d'en HAUT
10.25 am	37	6 HE	HEM
12.5 pm	37	1 HE	Working party H4 D5/9
4.25 pm	37	10 HE	BOIS d'en HAUT

B

10.a.m.	4.2" How	10 HE	SUZANNE, from direction of HEM
10.30 a.m	light fd. gun	10 Shr	MARICOURT WOOD, true bearing from A16 B9/1 115°
11.20 am	light fd gun	20 Shr	MARICOURT WOOD, from direction of GUILLEMONT
1.45 pm –4.0 pm	5.9" How	60	18, 19, 20 Trenches direction BOIS de VAUX – BOIS de HEM
3.10 pm	4.2" How		34, 35 Trenches from direction of GUILLEMONT
3.10 pm	light fd gun	4	34 from the Bois de BERNAFAY
3.30 pm	4.2" How	—	MARICOURT WOOD from GUILLEMONT

S.D. Bulteel
Lt RFA
for Rt. Grp.

Daily Report. 26/7/15.

A.

Time.	Bty.	No. of rounds fired	TARGET.
11.30 a.m.	119	2 A	working party in listening post Chapeau de Gendarme
1.40 p.m.	119	5 A	Hostile Battery FERME ROUGE, Retaliation
6.15 p.m.	119	2 A	Listening post Chapeau de Gendarme
9.0 p.m. – 9.45 p.m.	119	3 A	Single rounds at various intervals on Listening Post at Chapeau de Gendarme to prevent work being done
12.5 p.m.	120	25 A	to verify Registers on points opposite trenches 29 & 30
11.35 a.m.	123	21 A 1 AX	wire in front of Y wood
9.45 a.m.	124	10 A	BOIS d'en HAUT, Retaliation } for shelling of MARICOURT WOOD
9.50 a.m.	124	12 A	BOIS d'en HAUT, Retaliation } for shelling of MARICOURT WOOD
3.53 a.m.	124	6 A	Opposite 18 Trench, Retaliation

B.

Time.	Bty.	No. of rounds fired	TARGET.
~~9.35 a.m. – 9.45 a.m.~~	~~light fd gun~~	~~abt. 20 A~~	
9.36 a.m.	light fd gun	10 A	~~firing for~~ MARICOURT WOOD, firing from A24 B 0/6
9.45 a.m.	light fd gun	10 A	MARICOURT WOOD, firing from FERME ROUGE.
3.45 p.m.	light fd gun	7 A	18 Trench. firing from wood A 24 A 4/6
1.30 p.m.	light fd gun	8 A	MARICOURT WOOD, firing from FERME ROUGE

Sgd. [illegible] Bullock
Adjt. RFA. Rt. Gp.

Daily Report 27 11/15.

C.

Time	Btty	No. of Rounds fired.	TARGET
12 n.m	119	150	Enemy's wire between A23a 8/2 & A22a 9/9.
2.45 P.M.	119	4.5 / 2 HE.	Trench at foot of Chapeau. Retaliati
5.30 P.M.	119	1	" " "
6.55 P.M.	119	1	" " "
8.10 P.M.	119	1	" " " "
9.35 P.M.	119	1	" " "
11.30 A.M.	120	8	Retaliation. Bois de Favière.
5.15 P.M.	120	10	Opposite 34 Trench at request of Infant
11.30 A.M.	123	6	Retaliation A 17 a 1.8.
3.5 P.M.	123	6	Pr. A 17 a 1.8.
3.50 P.M.	123	4 H.E.	Retaliation. ~~4.5a~~ Bois d'en Haut.
4.35 P.M.	123	4.5 / 2 H.E.	Opposite 28 Trench.
10.50 A.M.	124	10	Retaliation. Bois d'en Haut.
2.53 P.M.	124	17	" " " "
9.30 A.M.	37	2 H.E.	Small party A 2 a b 9.8. Snipers.
3.5 P.M.	37	3 H.E.	Retaliation. Trench at foot of Chapea
4.10 P.M.	37	13 H.E.	M. Gun opposite 29 Trench.

B.

Time	Gun	Rounds	Target
10.40 A.M.	L.F.G.	25	On 26 Trench from about A 24 b 0.6.
10.45 A.M.	77 m.m.	10	On Maricourt Wood from E.
11.26 A.M.	77 m.m.	6	On 28 Trench from E.
2.45 P.M.		6 H.E.	On Moulin de F. from direction of Hem.
2.50 P.M.	77 m.m.	20	Maricourt Wood.
3.45 P.M.	L.F.G.	17	Near 28 trench from about A 18 d 8.9.
5.5 P.M.	How.	6	Over 28 trench from N.E.

T. J. O'Brien Lt.
for Dr. group Cmd

Daily Report 28/12

A

Time	By	No of Rounds fired	TARGET.
1·25pm	119	2 A	working party listening post at foot of Chapeau de Gendarme
·43pm	119	1 A	working party as above.
·53a.m	120	2 A	Opposite 35 Trench to verify Range, Correction
B.			
10·20a.m	light fld gun	7 shs.	27 T28 Trenches from direction of FERME ROUGE
2·40pm	light fldgun	2 shs	Communication trench PERONNE Road from direction of wood A24 B 0/6.

Sgd Butters
S/ROA
Adj RA Grp.

Daily Report 29/4/15

A.

Time	Bty	No. of rounds fired	TARGET
4.53 pm	119	1 A	working party on Chapeau de Gendarme
5.30 pm	119	4 A	working party on listening post at foot of the Chapeau
6.15 pm	119	7 A	Transport on road A3 B, reported by Infantry
9.50 pm	119	1 A	listening post at foot of the Chapeau
11.50 am	120	4 A	To verify Range & Corrector
1.25 pm	120	6A 2AX	Opposite 32 Trench Retaliation
11.15 am	123	10 A	dug-outs between A 16 D 8/2 – A16 D 6/6
2.50 pm	124	7 A	new work in fire trench A 17 D 1/6
11.30 am	37	7 BX	Dug-outs at foot of Chapeau de Gendarme
10.52 pm	119	2 A	Listening post on Chapeau de Gendarme
4.12 a.m	119	4 A	working party on S.W. edge of Y wood as reported by Infantry

B.

1.15 pm	Light Fdgn	——	32, 33 Trenches

S.W. Bradfield
Sc RA
Adj R.A.G.J.S.

Daily Report 30/11/15

A.

Time	Bty.	No. of rounds fired	TARGET.
4.30pm	119	5 A	working party on listening post at foot of Chapeau
5.0pm to 7.0pm	119	12 A	Cross-roads A 30 B 6/7
7.0pm	119	2 A	working party on listening post at foot of Chapeau
7.5pm	119	9 A	Y wood as Infantry reported a relief was taking place.
8.10pm	119	2 A	working party on listening post at foot of Chapeau
.53pm	119	2 A	
	1		
5.0pm to 7.0pm	120	12 A	roads A 11 A 7/6 to A 11 B 2/9
0.15pm	120	4 A	enemy's M. Gun A 10 D 0/3
11.40a.m.	123	10A 4AX	Large dug-out at A 11 C 1/5
5.0pm to 7.0pm	123	12 A	Road A 17 B 2/7 to A 18 A 0/7
11.20 a.m.	124	4 A	Opposite 18 Trench, retaliation
7.10 pm	124	10 A	Y wood, Infantry having reported a relief was taking place
5.0pm to 7.0pm	124	12 A	Tracks A 18 B 3/3 to A 18 B 3/7
1.25pm	37	6 BX	New trench joining Chapeau to listening post.

B.

Time	Bty.	No. of rounds fired	TARGET.
11.10 am	light fd gun	7 A	18 Trench. True bearing taken from G 4 c 9/5 was 63°. This line passes through B 20 A 2/6

G. D. Butler
Lt RFA
Adj Rt Grp

97th Bde: RFA.
Vol 4

121/593

21st D

XCVII Bde. Diary for Dec., 1915, is missing.

A.J.B.

D/ XCVII
to 2nd Cdn. Div
on 5/12/15
to Whatt Bde.

21st Divisional Artillery.

97th BRIGADE R. F. A.

JANUARY 1916.

Instructions regarding War Diaries and Intelligence Summaries are contained in F. S. Regs., Part II. and the Staff Manual respectively. Title pages will be prepared in manuscript.

WAR DIARY
or
~~INTELLIGENCE SUMMARY.~~
(Erase heading not required.)

Army Form C. 2118.

XII

Place	Date	Hour	Summary of Events and Information	Remarks and references to Appendices
ARMENTIERES (FRANCE)	1916 Jan. 1st		Brigade still in same position as last month –	
			A Battery (attached for tactical purposes to 95' Brigade R.F.A.) C 20 d. 8.8	
			B " " " 94 " " C 36. b 9.9	
			C " " " 96 " I 9. c 5.9	
			(Map Reference. – C 36 N.W.)	
			Lieut. KAY-SHUTTLEWORTH Hon. L. U. (A/131 RA late D/97 RA) mentioned in despatches for good work at LOOS. (Sept 26 – Oct 1st 1915)	
	" 11		Brigade took part in wire cutting at PONT BALLOT salient	
	" 14		Dr SHIMMIN (A/131 RA late D/97 RA) awarded Distinguished Conduct Medal for Conspicuous gallantry at LOOS. (Sept 26 – Oct 1st 1915)	
	" 22		2Lieut T. B. M. BROWN (S.R.) joined from England (attached) & attached to A/97 for instruction	
	" 24		Brigade took part in Bombardment of enemy trenches round FRELINGHIEN and PONT BALLOT Salient –	

2353 Wt. W2544/1454 700,000 5/15 D. D. & L. A.D.S.S./Forms/C. 2118.

Instructions regarding War Diaries and Intelligence Summaries are contained in F. S. Regs., Part II. and the Staff Manual respectively. Title pages will be prepared in manuscript.

WAR DIARY
or
INTELLIGENCE SUMMARY.
(Erase heading not required.)

Army Form C. 2118.

XIII

Place	Date	Hour	Summary of Events and Information	Remarks and references to Appendices
ARMENTIERES (FRANCE) JANUARY 1916	28		Capt C. A. G. O'MALLEY proceeded to ENGLAND for posting to Home Establishment	
	31		Brigade remain in position as under	
			"A" Battery (attached for tactical purposes to 95 Brigade RFA) C 20 d. 3. 8	
			"B" " " " " 94 " " C 26 b 9. 9	
			"C" " " " " 96 " " I 9 c 5. 9	
			Map Reference FRANCE C 36 N.W.	
			Total Expenditure of Ammunition during month HE 2088 rds Shrapnel 2051 rds	
			Casualties during month NIL	
			Edward Pollington Lieut Col RA Cmdg 97 Bde RFA	

2353 Wt. W2544/1454 700,000 5/15 D. D. & L. A.D.S.S./Forms/C. 2118.

21st Divisional Artillery.

97th BRIGADE R. F. A.

FEBRUARY 1916.

Instructions regarding War Diaries and Intelligence Summaries are contained in F. S. Regs., Part II. and the Staff Manual respectively. Title pages will be prepared in manuscript.

WAR DIARY
or
INTELLIGENCE SUMMARY.
(Erase heading not required.)

~~Army~~ Form C. 2118.

XIV

Place	Date	Hour	Summary of Events and Information	Remarks and references to Appendices
ARMENTIERES (FRANCE)	1916 Feb 1st		Brigade in same positions.	
	" 2		2 men seriously wounded thro tampering with Enemy fuze	
	" 3		Lieut V Hermann evacuated thro fractured wrist (accidental not thro Service)	
	" 7		Sqmt Norman B.A.C commissioned & sent to Base	
	" 12		D/113 R F A 35 Division joined for duty	
			Brigade took part in minor operation shooting against Enemy Trenches at PONT-BALLOT Salient	
	" 15		Brigade took part in Bombardment of Enemy front line Trenches	
	" 16		Lieut de WEAL (T) attached for 2 weeks course of instructions	
	" 17		Brigade took part in Bombardment of Enemy front line Trenches	
	" 18		Brigade took part in minor operation - Bombardment of Enemy front line & Support trenches	
	" 19		Continuation of yesterdays programme	
	" 20		Completion of yesterdays programme one Howitzer out of action thro' premature one man wounded (slightly)	
	" 24		Brigade took part in minor operation against Enemy Trenches, destruction of machine gun emplacement - Railway salient - Port BALLOT Salient - BLACK REDOUBT and SPARROW NEST.	
	" 26		Lieut BEGG joined from 21 D.A.C & attached to C/97 RFA	
	" 28		D/113 R.F.A. rejoined 35th Division	

XV

2353 Wt. W2544/1454 700,000 5/15 D. D. & L. A.D.S.S./Forms/C. 2118.

XV

Army Form C. 2118.

WAR DIARY
or
INTELLIGENCE SUMMARY.

(Erase heading not required.)

Instructions regarding War Diaries and Intelligence Summaries are contained in F. S. Regs., Part II. and the Staff Manual respectively. Title pages will be prepared in manuscript.

Place	Date	Hour	Summary of Events and Information	Remarks and references to Appendices
ARMENTIERES (FRANCE)	1916 July 29		Lieut de Weal (I) returned to England.	
			Total expenditure of ammunition for month { Shrapnel rounds 79 / H.E " 3442.	
			Brigade remains in position as under:–	
			MAP-REFERENCE:– FRANCE SHEET C 36 N W.	
			"A" Battery (attached to 95' Bde RA for tactical purposes) C 20 d 8 8.	
			"B" " (attached to 94' Bde RA for tactical purposes) C 26 b 9 9	
			"C" " attached to 96 Bde RA for tactical purpose) I 9. c 5 9	

[signature] Lieut. Col. R.F.A.
Commanding 97 Bde R.F.A.

2353 Wt. W2544/1454 700,000 5/15 D. D. & L. A.D.S.S./Forms/C. 2118.

21st Divisional Artillery.

97th BRIGADE R. F. A.

MARCH 1916.

Army Form C. 2118.

Sheet 16

WAR DIARY

~~or~~

~~INTELLIGENCE SUMMARY~~.

(Erase heading not required.)

Instructions regarding War Diaries and Intelligence Summaries are contained in F. S. Regs., Part II. and the Staff Manual respectively. Title pages will be prepared in manuscript.

97th Brigade R.F.A.

Place	Date	Hour	Summary of Events and Information	Remarks and references to Appendices
ARMENTIERES	1.3.16		Batteries of the Brigade still in the same positions.	
	7.3.16		Capt T. W. H. TACON was posted to A Battery and joined the same day.	
	9.3.16		Driver HARRISON of C Battery on filing out of wagon line mounted was badly wounded by enemy 77mm shell and died shortly afterwards.	
	13.3.16		Capt. E. H. PLACE R.F.A. commanding Brigade Ammunition Column was admitted to hospital.	
	14.3.16		Capt. F. REPEN adjutant of the Brigade was posted to Brigade Ammunition Column in command and joined the same day. Lieut A. REID R.F.A. of A Battery was appointed acting adjutant.	
			2. Lieut T. B M. BROWN went to Second Army Trench Mortar School for a course of instruction. Two 120 m.m. shells (one blind) struck C Battery's officers' billet - no casualties	
	18.3.16		2. Lieut R. G. BEGG R.F.A. was sent to Second Army School of Gunnery BERTHEN for a course of instruction.	
			Gunner KNIGHT of C Battery was accidentally wounded whilst cleaning an officer's revolver.	
			In the afternoon 1 section of C Battery was relieved by 1 section of D/81 RHA (17th Division) and moved out to rest area at W. 1. d. 5. 9 (Sheet 27 1/40,000)	
	19.3.16		C Battery (less 1 section) was relieved by ~~the How~~ D/81 (less 1 section) and joined the other section in the rest area.	
	21.3.16		Brigade Ammunition column was relieved by 81st B A C. and moved out to rest area at V. 6. a 8. 2. (Sheet 27)	

2353 Wt. W2544/1454 700,000 5/15 D. D. & L. A.D.S.S./Forms/C. 2118.

Instructions regarding War Diaries and Intelligence Summaries are contained in F. S. Regs., Part II. and the Staff Manual respectively. Title pages will be prepared in manuscript.

Army Form C. 2118.

WAR DIARY
or
~~INTELLIGENCE SUMMARY~~.
(Erase heading not required.)

97th Brigade R.F.A — Sheet 17.

Place	Date	Hour	Summary of Events and Information	Remarks and references to Appendices
ARMENTIERES	22.3.16		1 Section of A Battery and 1 section of B Battery were relieved by 1 section each of C/81 and B/81 respectively and moved to rest area – A Battery at V.5.c.4.1 and B Battery to V.6.c.5.2	Sheet 27 (1/40000)
	23.3.16		The relief of A and B Batteries was completed. The two batteries joining their sections in their respective positions in the rest area.	
			Brigade H.Q. was relieved by H.Q. 81st Bde. and moved to rest area at P.34.d.0.5. (Sheet 27)	
			During this relief the guns of this Brigade were left in their respective battery positions and the guns of the 81st Brigade were taken over by the 97th Brigade on arrival in the rest area. These guns taken over from the 81st Brigade have been found to be much worn and in need of a thorough overhaul before use.	
			The ammunition expenditure for the month of March up to the time of relief was 9 Shrapnel, 1400 H.E.	
near HAZEBROUCK	24.3.16		Lieut R.L. NASH R.F.A., having been appointed adjutant of the brigade, joined for duty.	
	30.3.16		Orders having been received for the Brigade to move (with the division) into the Fourth Army area a billetting party was sent forward. This party entrained at CASSEL and detrained at LONGUEAU near AMIENS – travelling with A/94th Brigade R.F.A. From this point the party travelled on cycles to the village of DAOURS arriving at 11 p.m. (10 miles due East of AMIENS)	

2353 Wt. W2544/1454 700,000 5/15 D. D. & L. A.D.S.S./Forms/C. 2118.

Instructions regarding War Diaries and Intelligence Summaries are contained in F. S. Regs., Part II. and the Staff Manual respectively. Title pages will be prepared in manuscript.

97 ... BRIGADE Date ... FIELD ARTILLERY

WAR DIARY
or
INTELLIGENCE SUMMARY.

(Erase heading not required.) Sheet 18.

Army Form C. 2118.

Place	Date	Hour	Summary of Events and Information	Remarks and references to Appendices
HAZEBROUCK	31.1.16		Brigade H.Q moved to new area and took up billet and office in RUE N'APOD, DAOURS, having entrained at CASSEL and detrained at LONGUEAU.	

H G Boyd [illegible] Lt Col R.F.A

Comm 97th Bde R.F.A

2353 Wt. W2544/1454 700,000 5/15 D. D. & L. A.D.S.S./Forms/C. 2118.

21st Divisional Artillery.

97th BRIGADE R. F. A.

APRIL 1916

Instructions regarding War Diaries and Intelligence Summaries are contained in F. S. Regs., Part II. and the Staff Manual respectively. Title pages will be prepared in manuscript.

97th BRIGADE No. Date R.F.A.

WAR DIARY or INTELLIGENCE SUMMARY.

(Erase heading not required.)

XXI (21) (8)

Army Form C. 2118.

97 RFA 19

Vol 8

Place	Date	Hour	Summary of Events and Information	Remarks and references to Appendices
DAOURS	1/4/16		A, B & C Batteries moved to new area. Entraining point CASSEL detraining point LONGUEAU	
	2/4/16		Batteries went into billets at VECQUEMONT adjoining DAOURS. The Brigade	
	3/4/16 to 6/4/16		Training and resting.	
	28/3/16		2/Lieuts. J.G. HARDING and D. TEGETMEIER joined the Brigade at Rest Area HAZEBROUCK (from Res. Brigade BALLINCOLLIG	
	7.4.16	1.30pm	1 Section of C Battery moved up to position already constructed at E.11.b.10.4. In this position they came under the 14th Bde. R.H.A. Group.	Sheet 62 d N.E 1/20000
	9.4.16		B. Battery commenced the construction of position at F.13.c.5.8 - 20 gunners being lent by A Bty to assist	"
	14.4.16		A Battery commenced work on new position at F.2.c.1.3	
	22.4.16		Construction of advanced Brigade H.Q. was started at F.19.a.2.4. a tunnel being made in a bank alongside a road.	
	30.4.16		Brigade H.Q. moved forward to advanced Wagon line at DERNANCOURT, E.21.c.6.4	

[signature] Lt. Col. R.F.A.
Comm. 97th Bde. RFA

2353 Wt. W2544/1454 700,000 5/15 D. D. & L. A.D.S.S./Forms/C. 2118

21st Divisional Artillery.

97th BRIGADE R. F. A.

M A Y 1 9 1 6

Instructions regarding War Diaries and Intelligence Summaries are contained in F. S. Regs., Part II. and the Staff Manual respectively. Title Pages will be prepared in manuscript.

WAR DIARY
or
~~INTELLIGENCE SUMMARY~~
(Erase heading not required.)

MAY Vol 9 — Army ~~Form C. 2118~~

97 RFA

Place	Date	Hour	Summary of Events and Information	Remarks and references to Appendices
DERNAN-COURT.	May		The work of battery-position construction was greatly hampered by the difficulty of obtaining R.E. material. To take an instance – during the first days of construction only 500 sand bags per day were available at the dump for the whole D.A.	
	2.		Remainder of "C" Battery moved to Wagon Line at DERNANCOURT.	
	11		B.A.C. transferred to Div. Col.	Ry: Map 62d NE 1/20,000
	14		CAPT REPEN & 2/LT TEGETMEIER, being surplus to establishment, were temporarily attached to this Brigade	
	11		"C" Battery relieved one section of 55th Bty at E.12.a.1.6 at 9 pm	
	12		Remaining section of "C" Battery relieved. Guns were exchanged, ammunition handed over & "C" Batt. placed under tactical command of 94th Group.	
	17.		2/LT TEGETMEIER proceeded to HAVANAS for Course of Instruction in TRENCH MORTARS.	
	20		Reorganisation of Brigade – A/97 becoming D/95. A/95 became A/97 preparing position at F.1.b.70.36. B/97 " D/94 while B/94 " B/97 in action at F.19.a.45 (under 94th Group). C/97 " D/96 C/96 " C/97 with 1 section in action at F.7.a.0.4 (under 96th Group) and " E.11.a.3.7 (" 94th ") and preparing position at F.7.b.3.5.	
	22,		Lt. J.R. Greig AVC transferred to Div Train Lt. Wall AVC attached to 97/RFA. Construction of Bde Battle HQ discontinued, and work on Div. OP continued till end of month.	
	27.		A/97 relieved C/95 at E.12.b.63 (Counter Battery Group).	
	28.		C/95 relieved B/97 at F.19.a.4.5. (under tactical command of 95th Group).	
	31.		2/Lt. TEGETMEIER rejoined Brigade	

Edward Pollinger. Lt Col RFA
Comd. 97th Bde RFA.

1875 Wt. W593/826 1,000,000 4/15 J.B.C. & A. A.D.S.S./Forms/C. 2118.

21st Divisional Artillery.

97th BRIGADE R. F. A.

J U N E 1916

97th Bde R.F.A.

Army Form C. 2118

Instructions regarding War Diaries and Intelligence Summaries are contained in F. S. Regs., Part II. and the Staff Manual respectively. Title Pages will be prepared in manuscript.

WAR DIARY
or
INTELLIGENCE SUMMARY
(Erase heading not required.)

579

Place	Date 1916	Hour	Summary of Events and Information	Remarks and references to Appendices
DERN[illegible]	Jan 3		Lieut TEGETMEIER attached to "A" 97 R.F.A.	
	5		New Battle H.Q. commenced at F 7 a 6.3. Map ref. 62 D NE 1/10000	
	13	9.5pm	One section "A" Bty moved from E 12 b 6.3 to F 13 b 7036 at 9.5 pm taking their guns from wagon line	
	13	6pm	One section "B" relieved one section "A" Bty at E 12 b 7.3. – Guns exchanged	
	14	9.5pm	Remainder of "A" Bty moved to new position – taking guns from wagon line	
	14	6pm	Remainder of "B" Bty moved from wagon line to relieve "A" 97 at E 12 b 7.3. ~~guns exchanged~~	
	14		"C" Bty taking their guns with them moved to F 7 b 3853 – one section from E 12 & the other from F 7 a.	
	15		Bde Battle H.Q. at F 7 a 6.3 abandoned – falls having taken place 6 times this is attributable to continuous wet weather & to the failure of the R.E. to supply the requisite material	
	15		New Bde. Battle H.Q. commenced at F 7 a 0505. ~~[illegible]~~ work proceeding with day & night.	
	16		Unloading of ammunition at Batteries began this night	
	17		Bde H.Q. moved into Battle H.Q. at F 7 a 0505 – Dressing station for Brigade established at same point	
	22		Bde O.T. established at F 7 d 8 5	

Continued Sheet 77

Wt. W593/826 1,000,000 4/15 J.B.C. & A. A.D.S.S./Forms/C. 2118.

Army Form C. 2118.

WAR DIARY
or
INTELLIGENCE SUMMARY.

(Erase heading not required.)

Instructions regarding War Diaries and Intelligence Summaries are contained in F. S. Regs., Part II. and the Staff Manual respectively. Title pages will be prepared in manuscript.

Sheet 38

580

Place	Date	Hour	Summary of Events and Information	Remarks and references to Appendices
	1916 June 23		21st Art. O.O. 22 received. Brigade in position at following points to take part in Anglo-French operation on the SOMME	Map Albert 62D N.E. 1/20000
			(1) Bde. H.Q. F 7 a 05 05	
			(2) A Battery. F 1 b 75 36	
			(3) B Battery E 12 b 7 3	
			(4) C Battery F 7 b 3 5	
			Wagon Lines at DERNENCOURT at E 21 c 6 4.	
	24 — 30	midnight	1000 rounds per gun dumped at Batteries	
			Brigade co-operated in bombardment as per 21 Div Art O.O. No 22 attached. A 3rd Infantry Brigade officer [illegible] report that they were satisfied that the [illegible] had been sufficiently destroyed.	[illegible] 1/20000
			Expenditure of Ammunition from 24–30th 18 pdr 11946 A – 6013 AX.	
			Casualties — Officers nil; O.R. Killed nil. Wounded 3	
			So far the equipment has stood the test well [illegible]. B.C.s report that guns are still shooting accurately.	

Lieut Col. R.A.
Comdg 97 Bde R.F.A.

4333 Wt W4344/1454 700,000 5/15 D. D. & L. A.D.S.S./Forms/C. 2118.

"A" Form. Army [illegible]

MESSAGES AND SIGNALS. No. of Message

Prefix .... Code .... m.	Words	Charge	This message is on a/c of:	Recd. at .... m.
Office of Origin and Service Instructions.	Sent		.... Service.	Date
	At .... m.			From
	To			
	By		(Signature of "Franking Officer.")	By

TO { Wire Cutting Zones

* Sender's Number	Day of Month	In reply to Number	AAA

A. Bty.	X. 20 d. 7 2	–	X. 26 b.	88.75
C "	X. 26. b. 88.75	–	X. 26. b.	85.40
B "	X. 27. b. 0.1	–	Dingle (inc)	X. 21. d. 3.1
" "	X. 27. b. 0.2	–	X. 27. a.	95.35
C "	X. 27. a. 95.35	–	X. 27. a.	60.45
A "	X. 27. a. 60.45	–	X. 27. a.	35.70
B "	X. 27. b. 1.7	–	X. 27. a.	35.80
A "	X. 26. b. 8.2	–	X. 27. a.	00.45
C "	X. 27. b. 7.4	–	X. ~~27~~ 21 d.	7.1

From

Place

Time

The above may be forwarded as now corrected. (Z)

Censor. Signature of Addresser or person authorised to telegraph in his name

* This line should be erased if not required.

3991.-W. & S. Ltd. London.-W 14142/641-90,000-4/15. Forms C 2121/10.

A Batty
A
C

Reference Instructions for Offensive No. 3

Change of Tasks

Task [illegible] will be undertaken by A instead of C Bty

[illegible]	A	instead of	C Bty
[illegible]	C	"	A
[illegible]	A	"	C
78	C	"	A
92	C	"	A

Task 89 A Battery will continue to cut wire or undertake any task which the Bde Comd considers advisable.

Correction

In Para 11 (c). The times therein given for concentrated bombardments should be one hour earlier – this will then agree with times given in tables.

Special Amendment

On nights X/Y and Y/Z, A/97 and C/97 will not fire between the hours of 11.30 p.m. and 1.30 a.m.

R. [illegible]
Lieut. R.F.A.
Adjutant, 97th Brigade R.F.A.

21st Divisional Artillery.

97th BRIGADE R. F. A.

J U L Y 1916.

Army Form C. 2118

Instructions regarding War Diaries and Intelligence Summaries are contained in F. S. Regs., Part II. and the Staff Manual respectively. Title Pages will be prepared in manuscript.

WAR DIARY
or
INTELLIGENCE SUMMARY
(Erase heading not required.)

Place	Date	Hour	Summary of Events and Information	Remarks and references to Appendices
			581	
			War Diary for July destroyed by Shell Fire.	
			[illegible] Lt RGA Adj. 97th Bde RGA	

1875 Wt. W593/826 1,000,000 4/15 J.B.C. & A. A.D.S.S./Forms/C. 2118.

21st Divisional Artillery.

Broken up 30th August; batteries distributed between 94th & 95th Brigades R.F.A.

97th BRIGADE R. F. A.

A U G U S T 1 9 1 6

Instructions regarding War Diaries and Intelligence Summaries are contained in F. S. Regs., Part II. and the Staff Manual respectively. Title pages will be prepared in manuscript.

WAR DIARY
or
INTELLIGENCE SUMMARY.
(Erase heading not required.)

Army Form C. 2118.

Sheet 28

Place	Date	Hour	Summary of Events and Information	Remarks and references to Appendices
DENIER	1/8/16		Orders were received to move up to the ARRAS area to relieve 14th Div. Art.	
	2/3/8/16		21st Div Art relieved 14th Div Art by section and single guns (in case of detached sections)	Append
			A/97 came under 95th Brigade Group for tactical purposes	
			C/97 " " 94th "	
			B/97 (less 1 sect) " " 94th " " "	
			" 1 sect " " 96th " " "	
			Batteries continued to be under 97th Bde HQ for administration	
	4/8/16		HQ 97th Bde relieved HQ 49th Bde at WANQUETIN	
			Lt Col POTTINGER was appointed TOWN COMMANDANT WANQUETIN with Lt RIEPEN as TOWN MAJOR	
WANQUETIN	10/8/16		2/Lieut FARRELL (A/97) admitted to hospital suffering from trench fever.	
	25/8/16		Lt Col POTTINGER RFA left to take over command of 283rd Brigade R.F.A.	
	28/8/16		Major M R C NANSON R.G.A (B/97) 2/Lieut LANKTREE (B/97) and Lieut T B	
			McLEROTH R.F.A left to join 11th Div Art.	
	29/8/16		Reorganization of 21st Div Art ordered	
	30/8/16	9 a.m.	Reorganization completed.	
			A/97 became A/95	
			B/97 (less 1 sect) joined A/94 to make 6 gun battery	
			1 sect " B/94 " " "	
			C/97 (less 1 sect.) " C/94 " " "	
			1 sect " C/95 " " "	

Instructions regarding War Diaries and Intelligence Summaries are contained in F. S. Regs., Part II. and the Staff Manual respectively. Title pages will be prepared in manuscript.

WAR DIARY
or
INTELLIGENCE SUMMARY.
(Erase heading not required.)

Army Form C. 2118.

Sheet 29.

R.F.A. Date

97th BRIGADE R.F.A. No. Date

Place	Date	Hour	Summary of Events and Information	Remarks and references to Appendices
WANQUETIN	31/8/16		Lieut. F REPEN R.F.A attached to 21st Div. Art. (H.Q.). LT NASH assumed duties of TOWN MAJOR Adjutant, Ord. off, and H.Q. staff only (N.C.O's + men) left.	

R. [signature] Lieut. R.F.A.
Adjutant, 97th Brigade R.F.A.

#353 Wt. W2544/1454 700,000 5/15 D. D. & L. A.D.S.S./Forms/C. 2118.

"A" Form. Army Form C. 2121.

MESSAGES AND SIGNALS. No. of Message

Prefix ... Code ... m.	Words	Charge	This message is on a/c of:	Recd. at ... m.
Office of Origin and Service Instructions.	Sent		... Service.	Date ...
	At ... m.			From ...
	To ...			
	By ...		(Signature of "Franking Officer.")	By ...

TO 94th. Bde. 95th.Bde 96th.Bde 97th.Bde Div. Col.

Sender's Number	Day of Month	In reply to Number	AAA
S.C. 60.	1st.		

[illegible]e instructions for relief No.1. forwarded under RM. 45 dated 31/7/16 hold good with the exception that Relief will take place on nights 2/3 & 3/4th. instead of on nights 3/4 & 4/5aaa Sections will march early to-morrow morning under Brigade arrangements from present Wagon Lines to New Wagon Lines aaa Brigades will occupy temporary Wagon Lines as follows 94th. 96th. and 97th. Bdes at WANQUETIN 95th.Bde at LATTRE ST. QUENTIN until completion of relief when they will move into Wagon Lines at present occupied by 14th. Divisional Artillery at the same places aaa Brigades should send forward Officer in advance of sections to-morrow morning to ascertain position of temporary Wagon Wagon Lines from their opposite numbers aaa Brigades will report to-night number of guns received back from Workshops aaa

From
Place
Time

Page 2.

The above may be forwarded as now corrected. (Z)

Censor. Signature of Addressor or person authorised to telegraph in his name.

* This line should be erased if not required.

T. & W. & J. M. Ltd., London. W 14042/M44. 75,000 12/15. Forms C 2121/10.

N 121

A Batt.
B
C

1. Remaining sections of Batteries of 97th Brigade RFA will march to WANQUETIN tomorrow starting at 8.30 a.m. There will be an interval of 10 minutes between hour of starting of each section.

2. Order of March
A Battery leading
B
C

[illegible]

17/11 Adj 97th Bde RFA

A Battery [illegible]
B
C

I

With reference to Instructions for Relief No. 1 :—

1. ~~Batteries~~ Relieving sections and guns will march to wagon lines WANQUETIN tomorrow morning.

Units will march at intervals of 15 minutes starting at 5.30 a.m.

Order of march

C Battery
A "
B "

2. Batteries will either send gun teams direct to HADARCQ to fetch guns or will send from wagon lines on arrival, at the discretion of Battery Commanders.

3. Further details will be issued later.

[illegible]

1/8/16 Adjt 91st Bde RFA

Secret

21st. D.A. No. B.M. 45.

N. 6444 1/8/16

INSTRUCTIONS FOR RELIEF NO. 1

The 21st. Divisional Artillery will relieve the 14th. Divisional Artillery, now covering I, J, and K. Sectors.

2. I Sector extends approximately from M.10 to the River Scarpe and is covered by BROWELL'S GROUP, under 11th. Division

J Sector extends approximately from River Scarpe to A.30.C.50 is held by 62nd. and 110th. Brigades, and covered by BOYCE'S GROUP.

K Sector extends approximately from A.30.C.50 to A.16.d.0.0., is held by 64th. Brigade, and is covered by OSBORNE'S GROUP.

3. 96th. Brigade and 1 Section of 97th. Brigade will relieve BROWELL'S GROUP

94th. Brigade and 1 Battery and 1 Section of 97th. Brigade will relieve BOYCE'S GROUP

95th. Brigade and 1 Battery 97th. Brigade, will relieve OSBORNE'S GROUP.

4. Relief will take place by Sections, and single guns on nights of 3/4th. and 4/5th. August, in accordance with Table "A"

5. On 2nd. August following Officers will visit the Units they are destined to relieve. Officers Commanding, 2 telephonists of 94th, 95th, and 96th, Headquarters, also Battery Commanders Signalling Officer or Senior Subaltern with 2 telephonists per Battery. 3 Motor busses will call at all Bde. Headquarters on 2nd. inst., starting with 94th. Bde at 7 am, and proceeding to 95th. 96th. and 97th. Brigades.

The Officers and N.C.Os. of the 95th. Bde. will go to the wagon lines of the 47th. Bde. at LATTRE St. QUENTIN. Remaining Officers and men will go to wagon lines of 46th. 48th. and 49th. Bdes at WANQUETIN. 14th. Divisional Artillery have arranged for guides and horses to meet these Officers at these wagon lines and to convey them to their destinations.

Brigade Commanders will return to their present billets the same evening, their Officers and N.C.Os. will remain in new positions until the arrival of their Sections.

6. The relieving Sections and guns will march from present billets to their wagon lines early on the morning of relief, and will continue the march to new positions after dark.

7. Instructions will be issued by 14th. Divisional Artillery as to times of relief etc. Brigade Commanders will arrange with their opposite numbers all details (guides etc.) for the whole of their group.

8. The limbers and wagons of 14th. D.A. will march out full They will be filled from limbers and wagons of 21 D.A. on arrival in wagon lines. Units will take over the Ammunition dumped at the guns.

9. Command of Divisional Artillery and groups will be assumed by the 21st. Divisional Artillery on completion of relief, on the morning of the 5th. inst.

10. Headquarters of 21st. Divisional Artillery will relieve Headquarters of 14th. Divisional Artillery at DUISANS on the morning of the 5th. instant.

11. The Divisional Column will move to MONTENESCOURT on the 4th. instant.

12. Acknowledge.

K Craig

Captain. R.A.

31st. July 1916. Brigade Major, 21st. Divisional Artillery.

Table "A".

95th. Brigade Group.

Night of	21st. D.A. Unit.	14th. D.A. Unit.	Position.	Remarks
4/5	95th. Bde HQ.	47th.Bde HQ.	G.22.c.90.65.	
3/4	A. 95th. Bde.	A. 47th. Bde.	G.15.c.9.3.	1 Section.
4/5	A. 95th. Bde.	A.47th. Bde.	G.15.c.9.3.	1 Gun.
4/5	A. 95th. Bde.	A. 47th. Bde.	G.16.b.55.60.	1 Gun.
3/4	B. 95th. Bde.	B. 47th. Bde.	G.15.d.8.5.	2 Guns.
4/5	B.95th. Bde.	B. 47th. Bde.	G.15.d.8.5.	1 Gun.
4/5	B. 95th. Bde.	B. 47th. Bde.	G.16.a.15.60.	1 Gun.
3/4 & 4/5	C. 95th. Bde.	C. 47th. Bde.	G.15.a.15.45.	1 Gun on each night
3/4 & 4/5	C. 95th. Bde.	C. 47th. Bde.	G.15.b.6.7.	1 Gun on each night.
3/4 & 4/5	D. 95th. Bde.	D. 47th. Bde.	G.8.d.50.15.	1 How on each night
3/4 & 4/5	D. 95th. Bde.	D. 47th. Bde.	G.16.c.20.95.	1 How on each night.
3/4 & 4/5	A. 97th. Bde.	B. 49th. Bde.	G.8.d.30.35.	1 Section on each night.

94th. Brigade Group.

Night of	21st. D.A. Unit.	14th. D.A. Unit.	Position.	Remarks
4/5	HQ. 94th. Bde.	HQ.46th. Bde.	G.21.d.20.45.	
3/4 & 4/5	A. 94th. Bde.	A. 46th.Bde.	G.15.d.3.0.	1 Section each night.
3/4 & 4/5	B. 94th. Bde.	B. 46th.Bde.	G.21.a.5.5.	1 Section each night.
3/4 & 4/5	C. 94th. Bde.	C. 46th.Bde.	G.15.d.8.3.	1 Gun each night.
3/4 & 4/5	C. 94th. Bde.	C. 46th.Bde.	G.21.b.7.8.	1 Gun each night.
3/4 & 4/5	D. 94th. Bde.	D. 46th.Bde.	G.15.b.55.55.	1 Section each night
3/4 & 4/5	1 Sect.B.97th.	1 Sect.C.49.	G.29.c.3.2.	1 Section each night
3/4 & 4/5	C. 97th. Bde.	C. 48th.Bde.	G.15.a.75.05.	1 Section each night

96th. Brigade Group.

Night of	21st. D.A. Unit.	14th. D.A. Unit.	Position.	Remarks
4/5	HQ. 96th.Bde.	HQ. 48th.Bde.	?	
3/4 & 4/5	A. 96th.Bde.	A. 48th.Bde.	G.20.d.55.40.	1 Section each night
3/4 & 4/5	B. 96th.Bde.	B. 48th.Bde.	G.20.d.5.8.	1 Section each night
3/4 & 4/5	C. 96th.Bde.	A. 49th.Bde.	G.26.a.9.1.	1 Section each night
3/4 & 4/5.	1 Sect.B97th	1 Sect.C49th	G.20.d.3.0. *	1 Gun each night.
3/4 & 4/5	D. 96th.Bde.	D. 48th.Bde.	G.27.c.7.7.	1 Section each night

* The Section at G.20.d.3.0. has been working with the battery at G.20.d.55.40. as a 6 gun battery.

21st Divisional Artillery.

Brigade broken up 30th August 1916.

H. Q. STAFF 97th BRIGADE R. F. A.

1st to 11th SEPTEMBER 1916.

97 th Brigade RFA

WAR DIARY
or
INTELLIGENCE SUMMARY
(Erase heading not required.)

Army Form C. 2118

21

Vol 13

Sheet 30

Instructions regarding War Diaries and Intelligence Summaries are contained in F. S. Regs., Part II. and the Staff Manual respectively. Title Pages will be prepared in manuscript.

Place	Date	Hour	Summary of Events and Information	Remarks and references to Appendices
WANQUETIN	1/9/16		2 Lieut. G E B POTTINGER (and Offr) left to join 283rd Bde RFA	
			Capt. M P PATON R.A.M.C left the Brigade.	
	8/9/16		H.Q transport was despatched to Advanced Horse Transport DEPOT, ABBEVILLE.	
	10/9/16		N.C.O's and men of H.Q Staff were despatched to the Base with the exception of 13 men posted to 94th and 95th Bdes and 21st D.A.C.	
	11/9/16		Lieut. R L NASH (adjutant) joined 95th Bde RFA	

R [illegible] Lt RFA
Adj 97th Bde RFA

1875 Wt. W593/826 1,000,000 4/15 J.B.C. & A. A.D.S.S./Forms/C. 2118.

www.ingramcontent.com/pod-product-compliance
Lightning Source LLC
Chambersburg PA
CBHW081537160426
43191CB00011B/1781
* 9 7 8 1 4 7 4 5 1 1 9 5 7 *